An

Invitation

to

Japan's Literature

An Invitation
to
Japan's Literature

Published

by

Japan Culture Institute

Senior Editors
   Tôhata Seiichi   President of Japan Culture Institute
   Agawa Hiroyuki   Novelist
   Edward G. Seidensticker Michigan University
   Murakami Hyôye   Managing Director of Japan Culture Institute
Compiled and Edited by
   Thomas J. Harper   Yale University
   William Currie   Sophia University
   Richard Wood   Earlham University
   David Tharp   Journalist
   Gotô Yumi   Japan Culture Institute
   Fujimori Shigeo   Japanese Painter
Published by **Japan Culture Institute**
Park Avenue 201, Sendagaya 1–20, Shibuya-ku, Tokyo
First printing   :   October 1974
ISBN: 0 – 87040 – 432 – 6   Printed in Japan

INTRODUCTION:
AN INVITATION TO JAPAN'S LITERATURE

THOMAS J. HARPER

There flourishes in Japan a genre of literary comment that so far as I know exists nowhere else in the world. Foreign readers — scholars, diplomats, journalists, clerics — are asked to describe what Japanese literature looks like from the outside, through foreign eyes; and so persistent is the demand for their opinions that hardly a week goes by but what some newspaper or magazine publishes a literary piece by a foreign writer, and on occasion whole issues of prominent journals have been given over to "blue-eyed" views of Japanese literature. This volume, too, has its beginnings in this peculiarly Japanese genre of criticism. Many of the essays collected here were originally published in Japanese translation in the *Tokyo Times*, and to these origins they owe much of their special character.

The authors represent a variety of nationalities and occupations seldom found in a volume of literary essays, and this in itself makes for a lively discussion. It is quite as enlightening to an American as to a Japanese to read a Spaniard's impressions of Watsuji's *Fûdo* (*Climate and Culture*); as it is to a scholar to read a diplomat's assessment of Shimazaki Tôson. And a question of great interest to any student of Japan — how the Chinese view the Chinese influences on Japanese literature — is the subject of Chen Shun-chen's essay on Bashô.

But there is still another quality that distinguishes many of these pieces, a curious combination of daring and earnestness; and this, I think, arises less from their cosmopolitan variety than from the common situation of their authors — that of the foreigner asked to write of Japanese literature for a Japanese audience. The writer is of course flattered to be asked; yet implicit in the request is a challenge. The sense of national isolation that produces this uneasy curiosity as to what foreigners may think of Japanese literature fosters at the same time a suspicion that their literature may lie at too great a remove from the literary experience of the rest of the world for an outsider ever to penetrate its depths. And so the foreign reader who is asked to hold forth in print on some aspect of Japanese literature senses that he is being asked not only to share his experiences of a work, but to justify his interest in it as well. He knows he must be on his mettle in a way that he might not were he writing for a less questioning audience. The essays in this volume are good examples of the vitality the situation engenders.

Jacques Pezeu begins his essay on the *Taketori Monogatari* (*The Tale of the Bamboo Cutter*) with a comparison of its themes with those of Western folklore, concluding that Princess Kaguyahime is "profoundly different" from her Western counterparts: she cannot fall in love with a human being. The point is an interesting one, but Mr. Pezeu's speculations on the reasons for the difference are even more arresting. "Could this be a reflection of Japanese pessimism?" he asks. "Man's destiny is a miserable one and is not attractive to a woman from another world. . . . Could it be that love in Japan is not strong enough for that?"

Edward Seidensticker approaches the *Genji Monogatari* (*The Tale of Genji*) through the endlessly argued question of authorship. For centuries scholars have debated whether the *Genji* was written by one or two or several persons. The question has inspired some ingenious theories (that the "Suma" and "Akashi" chapters came as divine revelation to the author, and inspired her to write the rest within the space of a few days), and some outrageous ones (that no woman could have written such a work without the help of a man); and the lack of conclusive evidence has kept the issue alive to the present day. Professor Seidensticker, too, offers an opinion in the matter, but in addition makes a suggestion that seems not to have occurred to many *Genji* scholars, and might raise the eyebrows of some — that ultimately it does not really matter how many Murasaki's there were; that should the question one day be settled, it will in no way alter the beauty of the novel. He tells us nothing of the novel itself, but the fascination of the debate is a stronger inducement to read the *Genji* than an expository piece of equal length could ever have been.

In his essay on the *Soga Monogatari* (*The Tale of the Soga Brothers*), Thomas Cogan points out what he considers a basic difference between the Japanese and the Western conception of the hero, namely the irrelevance of "right" and "wrong" in the legal sense, and the overwhelming importance of "selflessness." The literary implications of his assertion are considerable. Judged strictly on the basis of right and wrong, Suketsune, the villain of the tale, emerges as not altogether villainous, while the Soga brothers can no longer be regarded as paragons of virtue. Presumably further inquiry might reveal the same to be true of other "heroes" and "villains" of the medieval war chronicles, as for example Minamoto Yoshitsune or Kajiwara Kagetoki. As Mr. Cogan realizes, this need not cause us to lower our estimation of the *Soga Monogatari*. To rehabilitate Suketsune is not to destroy the heroic image of the vengeful brothers that vivifies the legend. Far from eroding the basis of our appreciation of the war chronicles, Mr. Cogan's observation adds a new dimension to our understanding of the heroes and villains they depict.

Discussion of the medieval dramatist Ze'ami tends to center upon the elusive critical term *yûgen* (mystery and depth) that occurs so frequently in his theoretical writings on the *noh*. Don Kenny achieves something of a tour de force in his essay on Ze'ami by never once mentioning the term. Drawing instead upon his own experiences as an actor and drama critic, he suggests that Ze'ami is best understood not simply as a theorist of the *noh*, but as a consummate actor, director, and writer as well – as a "total man of the theatre." That Ze'ami was all of these things is of course well known, but amidst all the talk of *yûgen* we may need to be reminded of it.

More recent works seem to elicit reactions of a slightly different sort than the classics, less an academic questioning of established literary opinion than a personal involvement with the culture of modern Japan. For the culture that produced the literature of the past hundred years or so is still very much alive, and the direct experience of that culture, in some cases for many years, has inevitably colored the essayists' experience of the works they discuss. The results are as much social as literary comment.

Margaret Yamashita, for instance, deplores as much as the injustices to women depicted by Higuchi Ichiyô the fact that modern Japan has yet to rectify many of these wrongs. Meredith Weatherby, on the other hand, tells of his close and rewarding friendship with Mishima Yukio that began when he made the first two translations of Mishima's novels. Čiháková Vlasta chides the older generation of Japanese readers for their insensitivity to the more precious aspects of Dazai Osamu's style; while Lawrence Redman takes the Western literary establishment to task for awarding the Nobel Prize to Kawabata Yasunari while Shimazaki Tôson's *Yoakemaye* (*Before the Dawn*) remains untranslated. And the noted film critic Donald Richie, in perhaps the most moving essay in the collection, relates with a mixture of elegiac regret and bitterness his feeling of affinity with Nagai Kafû, with whom he laments the victory of the cold and proper "Kano line" over the vital plebeian arts of Edo.

In short, different writers react to the challenge in different ways, some finding fault, some sympathizing, some propounding deliberately reactionary views, some hewing steadfastly to the "traditional" interpretation of a work. Seldom, though, does the situation produce a dispassionate analysis of the work under discussion. It brings out a side of the writer that may not always appear in the more comfortable circumstance of writing for his own countrymen; and whether this be for better or worse, the results are not often dull.

Not every essay in the collection is of this genre, of course. Some have been revised by their authors for publication here; and some were written especially for the volume: Professor Keene's on Chikamatsu Monzayemon, Dr. Mills's on *Konjaku Monogatari* (*Tales of Ages Ago*), and Mr. Melanowicz's on Kaikô Takeshi, to name only three. But if there is any single quality that sets the collection apart from others of its kind, it is that tone of a writer on his mettle that marks so many of the essays in the book, and indeed makes the book one that could only have been produced in Japan.

Such a collection cannot pretend to offer a comprehensive introduction to Japanese literature. The individual essays are too short to give more than a partial glimpse of the works and authors they treat of, and the audience for which many were written could be counted on to possess considerable knowledge of Japanese history and culture. Mr. Murakami's excellent "Brief History of Japan's Literature" will help the reader who lacks this background to place the works in their historical context. But then the aim of the book, as the title indicates, is not to "introduce," but to "invite" the reader to explore the literature of Japan on his own — to interest not only the new reader, but also to induce those long familiar with Japan's literature to reread and reconsider some of the works they already know — and in this the authors of these essays succeed admirably. One may not always agree with what they say, but the vigor and enthusiasm with which they approach their subject, inspired to some extent by the unique circumstances in which they wrote, is unquestionably contagious.

CONTENTS

Essays

A

Brief History

of

Japan's Literature

A Brief History of Japan's Literature

MURAKAMI HYÔYE

I   Ancient Literature

The Beginnings of Japanese Culture

If one views Japan macroscopically, one sees a single language, a single people, and what can be called a single form of national polity, continuing well over a thousand years. There is no comparable case in world history. If one considers the causes of this continuity, there is a strong link with the geographical location of Japan as a chain of islands standing in the Pacific Ocean off the east coast of Asia — close enough to receive cultural influence from the Continent, but too far for invasion.

Where did this island people, the Japanese, come from? Do the present inhabitants date back continuously to Stone Age times? These are riddles; however, to understand Japanese culture it is important to realize clearly that influences came both from Oceania — Malaysia and the Indonesian islands — and from the Continent — Nepal, Indo-China, China, Siberia, and Korea.

Excavations have shown that so-called *Yayoi* culture (second century, B.C. ~ third century, A.D.) was based on rice paddy cultivation, and there is no doubt that these people are the direct racial ancestors of the present Japanese. But to seek the origin of the Japanese, to try to understand their foundation prior to *Yayoi* culture, is to set an unsoluble problem. One can only guess whether the origin is in *Jômon* culture (10,000 B.C. ~ 200 B.C.), from which period there have been discoveries of the world's oldest existing earthenware.

Jômon period Japanese were a nut-gathering, hunting, and fishing people. The period name, *"Jômon,"* dates from 1879, when an American zoologist, E.S. Morse, excavated the "Shell Mounds of Ômori" in a Tokyo suburb. The earthenware found in them carried designs made with cord, hence it came to be called *Jômon* (meaning "cord-marked").

As the origins of Japanese culture are very ancient, so is the independence of the Japanese language. If one searches for family resemblances, the Korean language is a distant relative, but it is difficult to trace other ancestors. Among languages Japanese is practically an orphan.

Creation of the *Kojiki*

The oldest work written in Japanese — that is, the oldest extant work — is the *Kojiki*. If "literature" is what is written down in the symbols of a language, then Japanese literature begins with the *Kojiki*, which was completed in 712 A.D.

Not very long before that time, in the third and fourth centuries, the multiplicity of tribal units had been unified by the political power centered in Yamato (present-day Nara). At the end of the fourth century, Japan negotiated with, and fought a series of wars with, the nations on the Korean peninsula. From that point Japan experienced rapid development, brought about mainly by the large numbers of people who crossed over from Korea, bringing with them their advanced culture.

Chinese characters — *Kanji* — were introduced into Japan through Korea — according to tradition in the sixth century. But in fact it seems to have happened somewhat earlier. After writing came into use, by order of the imperial government the task of collecting and recording traditional legends, as well as contemporary conditions, was begun in the early seventh century. But since these records were lost, a new collection based on what remained of them was begun during the reign of the powerful Emperor Temmu (?-686). It was completed in the early eighth century, and is known as the *Kojiki* (*Records of Ancient Matters*).

The *Kojiki* is made up of three books. The contents of the first are the myths about the Creation and the legendary great-grandfather of the first emperor who was said to have descended from heaven, along with the gods, to the top of a mountain in Kyûshû. The second book tells about the first emperor's expedition from Kyûshû to Yamato (Nara), giving the myth of the creation of the ancient Japanese state. In addition it relates the heroic story of the son of the twelfth emperor, who fought pacification campaigns throughout Japan. These stories are not historical fact; however, they are studded with memories of actual events. Finally, the third book deals with the history and legends of the fifth and sixth centuries.

Something that strikes one as unusual when reading the *Kojiki* is that there is scarcely any description of wars or battles in the legendary tales about the formation of the Japanese state. Even in the best-known hero story — that of Yamato Takeru, there appears no battle scene in which valiant warriors fight, although it does contain descriptions of various schemes and stratagems. This feature is probably a reflection of actual history, for the state of Japan was most likely not unified through a single big war of conquest; rather, unification was achieved gradually through political negotiations — naturally including pressure — and politically expedient connections made through marriages. Since the Japanese were not cattle herders, but a group of farmers primarily cultivating rice, they did not undertake the carnage of a large-scale war.

The *Kojiki* is a treasure house of ancient Japanese legends, and it contains a rich harvest of songs (poems), through which the feelings of the Japanese of that time are transmitted.

Eight years after the *Kojiki*, the *Nihon Shoki* (*Chronicles of Japan*) was produced. Written in contemporary Chinese, it deals with the period from the age of the gods to the end of the seventh century. When it was written, the Chinese histories, *Records of the Historian* and the *History of the Former Han Dynasty*, had been introduced into Japan. Not to be outdone by these books, the history of Japan was compiled, apparently by imperial decree.

While the *Kojiki* was written introspectively in Japanese, the *Nihon Shoki* was written with a consciousness directed overseas, especially toward China. Details of the contents of the two books differ, but many parts of both use the same raw materials.

The year after the *Kojiki* was completed, the government ordered records of the various provinces' (*kuni*) histories, legends, and curious incidents, to be presented from all over Japan. Ranging from contemporary geography to local history, that book, when completed, was called the *Fudoki* (*Topographical Records*), but it has been scattered and lost for a long time, and now only a little remains of the original.

The Poets of the *Mannyôshû*

When one speaks of ancient Japanese literature, one cannot neglect the *Mannyôshû*. "*Mannyô*" means "ten thousand leaves," but the collection actually contains about four thousand five hundred poems.

It is not clear when the *Mannyôshû* was completed, but it seems to have been finished by the beginning of the Heian period (794). The poems, written by about two hundred sixty people, were composed between the fourth and eighth centuries. Contributors ranged from emperors, members of the imperial family, the nobility, and court poets to anonymous farmers from remote areas, soldiers, and housewives. The conspicuous strength of this collection derives from its exceptional and unforgettable poems, which have no relation to the status of their authors. Though it is not, strictly speaking, democratic, this collection shows that social class distinctions were transcended, at least in esthetic appreciation. Also, the fact that in ancient times even farmers and warriors could write beautiful poetry cannot be overlooked when one investigates Japanese culture.

While nearly half of the poems are by unknown authors, certain outstanding poets are represented by many poems. Since the poems of the *Mannyôshû* are based on lines of five and seven syllables, they indicate the original form of the Japanese *tanka* poetry.

Himgashi no
No ni Kagirohi no
Tatsu miete,
Kaheri mi sureba

Tsuki katabukinu.

> I could see the mist hovering over the eastern fields,
> But turning, there was the moon,
> Setting behind the western hills.

This poem is by Kakinomoto no Hitomaro, who is representative of the lyric poets. On the other hand, Yamanouye no Okura wrote often of the affection between parents and children, and about the life of the poor: so he is called "the poet of human life."

> More than that of gold, rather than silver,
> Over jewels or anything,
> The treasure that excells all,
> The treasure of one's children.

The poet with the most poems in the *Mannyôshû* is Ôtomo no Yakamochi. It is said that he was also the collection's editor.

As was mentioned above, rather than the kind of poetry written by court poets, that of anonymous rural people expresses eloquently the life and feelings of the common people of that time.

> Snowing on Tsukuba mountain?
> Or possibly not?
> Is her *kimono*
> Drying in the wind?

In reading the following poem, one can imagine the extension of control by the Nara imperial house into eastern Japan.

> The Emperor's command overawes;
> So I watch the rocky shore gliding by,
> Leaving father and mother.

II The Literature of the Heian Period

Development of *Kana*

At the end of the eighth century the Emperor Kanmu moved the capital from Nara to Kyoto. From then for a period of about four hundred years, we have what is called the Heian period until the twelfth century, when *Shôgun* Minamoto no Yoritomo established the *bakufu* (military government, literally "tent government") in Kamakura.

In the early years of this four hundred year period there was a rebellion on the northeastern frontier, and toward the end of this Heian period a struggle for supremacy developed between the rival military clans of Genji (Minamoto clan) and Heike (Taira clan). This struggle eventually brought war to the whole country. But aside from these two disturbances most of the Heian period saw continuous peace.

The court nobility in Kyoto led an elegant and pleasant daily life, strolling to look at cherry blossoms in the spring, maple leaves in the fall, and holding moon-viewing parties. The nobles exchanged *tanka* poems with their friends, and the sound of musical instruments could be heard continuously from the palaces. The Fujiwara family was especially closely related to the imperial family, and prospered greatly as court nobility. If one were to sum up Heian literature in one phrase, it would be the "literature of the nobility."

It must not be overlooked that the *kana* syllabary was developed during this period. Until then Japanese words were expressed in writing through the meanings of the Chinese characters, or their pronunciation. Since this was extremely inconvenient, the *kana* syllabary was contrived by simplifying Chinese characters. From around the ninth century women in the court generally wrote in *kana*. Through the fact that even women could write freely, they exerted great influence on the development of literature.

The Flourishing of Feminine Literature

Heian period literature was the literature of the nobility, and its most representative works are the *Tale of Genji* (*Genji Monogatari*) and other feminine writings. Why did feminine literature thrive at this time? There is no simple answer, but the following three reasons can be offered:

(a) There was a long period of peace in the country, under the government of the court of Kyoto. The court's prosperity, like that in the history of any country, was based on taxing the work of farmers, both their produce and a direct labor tax. The imperial government did not give much thought to military power, and for a long time had sufficient authority to govern Japan effectively. Included in this authority was a feeling of longing among rural people for the high culture of Kyoto. In time rural culture came to be an imitation of Kyoto style. This cultural authority, rather than naked power, can be seen to be relied upon widely during this Heian period. (b) At that time the status of women was high, because Japanese society still retained vestiges of the matrilineal family system. The overall high status of women was generally lost after the seventeenth century, that is, after the strong rule of the *bakufu* (military government) was established in Edo (Tokyo).

(c) Heian period nobles were zealous in imitating Chinese culture, and very proud of their Chinese learning. When they spoke of "talent," they meant knowledge of Chinese culture. (For a while, there was a corresponding phenomenon of imitations in post-Meiji Japan, when "knowledge" meant Western knowledge, and the developed culture of Europe was imported.) Of course, since the Heian nobility had inherited the tradition of the *Mannyôshû*, Japanese style poetry — *tanka* — thrived, and many excellent collections were made. But there was not much interest in writing prose. Here, armed with the weapon of *kana*, women writers appeared on the stage.

Diaries and Miscellanies

In the history of world literature, the richness of the Heian period of Japan deserves particular mention. The special coloration of this literature was provided by the superb diaries.

The first diaries were written by men, in *kanji* (Chinese characters), but then women began to write them in *kana*. Sometimes the diaries were filled with *tanka* poems. Among the famous diaries of the time was the *Tosa Diary* of Ki no Tsurayuki. It contains the statement, "Men write diaries; I too, a woman, will try writing." Here the author, pretending to be a woman, wrote using both *kana* and *kanji*. Thus it was in this period that the present Japanese practice of writing with a combination of *kana* and *kanji* began.

The Heian period had many women of genius who left outstanding diaries, among the best-known of which are the *Kagerô Diary* (by the mother of Fujiwara no Michitsuna), the *Izumi Shikibu Diary*, the *Murasaki Shikibu Diary*, and the *Sanuki no Suke Diary*.

One more genre of this period was the miscellany (*zuihitsu*). The term means "following the brush," with no particular theme. Rather, a kind of essay is built up from brief statements — one's views of events, occasional thoughts — through which can glimmer subtly the author's impressions of nature and his perspective on human life. This genre has become one of the special features of Japanese literary tradition, and many Japanese are still fond of writing and reading in it. It is because of this tradition of *zuihitsu* that Japanese readers value highly "I-novels," of which a great many are written.

Sei Shônagon's *Makura no Sôshi* (published in English as *The Pillow Book of Lady Sei Shônagon*) is known as a masterpiece, and a pioneering work in this genre. Particularly because of the richness of the sense with which it catches the (feminine) author's profound feeling for the seasons, for the seasonal beauty of nature, this book is one archetype of Japanese literature.

Of the tales written in *kana*, the oldest is said to be the *Taketori Monogatari*. Both author and date are unknown, but it is said to have been written about the beginning of the tenth century. It is popularly known as the *Kaguyahime no Monogatari*, after the name of its heroine. Influence from Chinese fairy tales can be seen in it, but this fanciful story is put together in an extremely interesting way. Murasaki Shikibu, authoress of the *Genji Monogatari*, called it the "oldest ancestor of the prose tales".

The *Ise Monogatari* was written about the same time. It is written in prose, into which are freely inserted poems by the famous poet Ariwara no Narihira. This style, too, became archetypical for Japanese literature.

Genji Monogatari (The Tale of Genji)

The *Genji Monogatari* is not only the representative masterpiece of Heian literature, but of ancient Japanese literature as well; moreover, it is a world-famous classic. The authoress, Murasaki Shikibu, was the daughter of Fujiwara no Tametoki. After the death of her husband she served the consort of the Emperor Ichijô. This empress was the daughter of Fujiwara no Michinaga. Michinaga is known as the leader of the Fujiwara clan at the peak of its prosperity during Heian times. The *Genji Monogatari* was a product of this Fujiwara prosperity, so it can be said to be the literature of affluence.

A long novel of fifty-four "books," the *Genji Monogatari* revolves around two heroes, Hikaru Genji and his son. Genji was an imperial prince, who was well-established as an outstanding, attractive, and talented man. Diverse women appear in their connections with the heroes. All together, some four hundred characters appear in the novel. That each of them is given a distinct individual character deserves our admiration.

This novel attained profundity through the way the literary genius of its authoress combined refined psychological insights cultivated through contemporary diary writing with the lyricism of the stories that mixed prose and poetry. While portraying elegant court life, this book reaches the deepest parts of the human psyche, and the indistinct pathos felt there is a reason why this ancient work is still read.

In the Edo period the scholar Motoori Norinaga said that the esprit of the *Genji Monogatari* is "*mono no aware*" (the *aware* of things). *Aware* is a Japanese expression used to express all sorts of emotions, especially deep feelings of fondness and sadness. He explains "*mono no aware*" as a sense born at a point of harmonious agreement, when the objective grasp of things and subjective emotions are unified.

To sum up, the appeal of the *Genji Monogatari* lies in its vivid, refined, and subtly sensitive descriptions of eternally unchanging human loves, passions, and desires, through detailed accounts of the elegant life of the Heian nobility, their customs and rituals. It seems almost a miracle that this great romance was written in the early eleventh century, six hundred years before Shakespeare, and three hundred years before Dante's *Divine Comedy*. At the same time, it suggests the richness of the cultural and literary climate of the Heian period.

The influence of the *Genji Monogatari* on Japanese culture in the centuries to follow has been both long and profound. In every age it has been read as a model, and even today there are uncountable "*Genji* study groups" all over Japan. One can also see the shadow of the *Genji Monogatari*, its influence, in the works of such writers as Higuchi Ichiyô, Tanizaki Jun'ichirô, and Kawabata Yasunari.

Though both are in the Orient, Japan unlike China, did not produce great thinkers such as Confucius and Lao-tsze, nor great historians such as Ssu-ma Chien, author of *Records of the Historian*. It was rather in the field of fiction that Japan had the glory of a world masterpiece.

Going from this literature of the nobility to the roughly contemporary *Konjaku Monogatari* can give the reader a jolt, for it is a sharply contrasting collection of raw episodes from the life of the masses. Since it was originally a collection of illustrative stories used by a priest in preaching, it is divided into 3 parts of Indian stories, Chinese stories, and Japanese stories respectively, and the part on Japan is further divided into a Buddhist section and a secular section. Though an ancient book it is still read with interest since the Japanese secular part includes such extraordinary stories as the one about the priest with an abnormally long nose, or that about the man whose wife was raped before his eyes. In his early period, Akutagawa Ryûnosuke sometimes took themes from this collection, and one of the stories was made into the famous film *Rashômon* by the director Kurosawa.

III Medieval Literature

The Rise of the *Bushi (samurai)*

The prosperity of even the Fujiwara, as well as their power, gradually declined while internal strife within the clan continued. The imperial family also joined in these disputes. The major difference between this and earlier struggles was that the *bushi* (warriors) moved into the role of major actors.

In the provinces as well, peace and order were disturbed and the farmers had to defend themselves by their own strength. The *bushi* emerged as central to this self-defense. The "Hôgen Rebellion" was a struggle in Kyoto. The major actors in this war were members of the Fujiwara and imperial families. Both Genji (Minamoto clan) and Heike (Taira clan), the two leading *bushi* clans, were involved, and members of these families fought among themselves as some of them aligned with each side. This war marked the end of the Heian period.

The Genji and Heike clans became involved in a struggle for supremacy which entrapped all Japan in war. The leader of the victorious Genji, Minamoto no Yoritomo, set up the *bakufu* in Kamakura in 1192. For the next four hundred years, until the Tokugawa clan opened an era of peace by establishing their *bakufu* in Edo (now Tokyo), we have what is called the "middle ages".

War Chronicles (*Gunki Monogatari*)

The first two war chronicles were called the *Hôgen Monogatari* and the *Heiji Monogatari*, after the wars they recounted. The best representative of these war chronicles is the *Heike Monogatari*, the tale of the brief supremacy and sudden downfall of the Heike clan. The *Heike Monogatari* relates various episodes during the period of prosperity of the Heike, and then goes on to describe, one by one, the various battles, in a tone at once heroic and tragic. In this period Buddhist thought spread to every corner of the land, so that a pervasive feeling for the transiency of life, as well as courage, flows through the story.

"Prosperity is sure to wane. He who boasts cannot last long. All is like a dream in a spring evening. The strong will eventually perish. All is as the dust blown before the wind." Through this well-known opening passage of the *Heike Monogatari*, aided by the eloquence of traveling minstrels relating it to the accompaniment of their *biwa* (Japanese lute), this story was spread widely among the Japanese. Even those who could not read could weep when they heard this story. For generations to come this tale of courage and of anguish was to have great and continuous influence on the Japanese spirit, especially on the "way of the warrior" (*bushidô*). Linked with the "*mono no aware*" of the *Genji Monogatari*, this Buddhist feeling of transiency deposited deep in the Japanese spirit a sense of resignation combined with a sense of compassion.

Among the many episodes in the *Heike Monogatari*, those which have received special emphasis from time to time are the ones that have images of valiant *bushi* who esteem honor, and of the human anguish that lies behind valor.

One other outstanding military chronicle was the *Taiheiki* (*Chronicle of Peace*) which tells of the long wars after the collapse of the Kamakura shogunate. At that time the imperial house was divided into northern and southern branches, and the country overrun by war, so the title of the chronicle is sarcastic. This tale, too, was spread widely by professional narrators.

Medieval Miscellanies

Inheriting the tradition of the *Makura no Sôshi* from Heian times, the middle ages saw a flowering of the literary miscellany (*zuihitsu*). Especially well-known are *An Account of My Hut* by Kamo no Chômei (1153-1216) and *Essays in Idleness* by Yoshida Kenkô (ca. 1283–ca. 1353).

"Water flowing in a stream does not cease, yet this water is not the same water as a second ago. When water becomes stagnant, bubbles float to the surface and burst, or, if they survive, do not last long. In this world it is the same for men and material things." To understand this quotation from *An Account of My Hut*, we need to realize that under these sentences flows the Buddhist feeling of the transiency of everything. *Essays in Idleness* was written by Yoshida Kenkô, a Buddhist writer, under the same influence: "As there is nothing for me to do (But actually he doesn't want to do anything.) I spend all day, writing down in haphazard fashion what comes into my mind, and I come to have a strange feeling." This opening sentence from the *Essays in Idleness* exactly expresses the author's attitude. The author, although abandoning the world, at the same time retains an interest in various things of the temporal life; by criticizing and abandoning things, at the same time he teaches the joy of life. The Japanese Buddhist sense of resignation, and a shrewd realism, live together in the people without contradiction. Perhaps this is a point at which Westerners find Japanese difficult to understand. This contradiction is not thought of as such, but if the contradiction were thrust before their eyes, the Japanese might reply, "Such is a human being."

An important feature of the development of this view of human life is that it came during the long periods of fierce war in the middle ages. Kamo no Chômei lived during the Genji-Heike wars: Yoshida Kenkô lived during the warfare when the imperial house was split into northern and southern factions.

Noh and *Kyôgen*

In the present as well, *noh* is the theater especially characteristic of Japan, and its form is about the same as it was halfway through the medieval period. There were two sources of its development: (a) dance in the presence of the gods, or with the gods, at *shintô* shrines; (b) dance offered in the fields as a prayer for an abundant harvest. These were synthesized by Kan'ami and his son Ze'ami (1362?–1443). Ze'ami was simultaneously a *noh* actor, director, and playwright. Among the many *noh* plays transmitted to the present, over thirty are definitely his. Moreover, he was an outstanding critic, writing about practice, performance, intonation, music, scenarios, play direction, and management. Many of his essays on esthetics have survived through the following centuries.

The scenarios on which the staged *noh* performance is based are called "*yôkyoku.*" These take their materials from historical events and legends, and by dressing them in sentences which are like beautiful silk garments, make the contents suggestive and symbolic. This esthetic ideal is sometimes called "*yûgen,*" a concept included in theories of Japanese literature. The ideal of *yûgen* is profound subtlety, something difficult to measure. Representing graceful refinement, *yûgen* stands for a profound artistic effect beyond word or expression.

During the same period, materials taken more directly from ordinary life were put into comedies called *kyôgen*, and these survive to the present.

IV The Literature of the Edo Period

The Revival of Scholarship and the Culture of the City-dweller (*chônin*)

The last half of the medieval period was a time of uninterrupted civil strife, especially during the eleven years following 1467 (the Ônin War). This war broke out in Kyoto itself, and signaled the collapse of the Muromachi period's Ashikaga *bakufu*. Throughout the country military commanders fought one another for hegemony. The period is known as "the period of warring states." This struggle was finally resolved by Tokugawa Iyeyasu, who emerged as the supreme leader of the country and established the rare phenomenon of three hundred years of peace.

The Tokugawa *bakufu*, settled in Edo Castle, promoted scholarship on a broad front as a means to preserve order in society. Chinese Confucianism became the core of the learning. The *bakufu* hoped that if people studied the teachings of Confucius and Mencius, they would come to serve their parents, have good manners, and honor their superiors. Thus, so-called "feudalistic ethics" were spread widely, and at the same time, through study at the "*juku*" (private schools of Confucian teachers), the level of general knowledge of farmers and merchants was raised dramatically.

On the other hand studies in the Japanese classics thrived among scholars side by side with Confucian learning. This scholarship was a re-examination of research in the Japanese classics, the *Kojiki*, the *Mannyôshû*, etc. As this research proceeded, people came to be aware that the imperial house was above the *bakufu*, a realization that was to contribute intellectual energy to the *bakufu's* overthrow.

Another phenomenon of the times was that though the *bushi* had, naturally, taken political power into their hands, gradually it was the merchants who became wealthy. Eventually the *bushi* had to borrow from them, so that the real power of the merchants increased. There came to flourish a "culture of urban citizens" (*chônin bunka*). This popular culture provided the basis for the modern culture that was to succeed it.

Birth of *Haiku* and Its Prosperity

Haiku is one of the major representative genres of Edo period literature. A *haiku* is composed of seventeen syllables, arranged in three phrases 5—7—5. If we trace its source, we are led back to the *Mannyôshû*.

The reader has already encountered the 5—7 syllabic rhythm in the *tanka* (*waka*) poems of the Heian and medieval periods, where the syllables were 5—7—5/7—7. Continued repeatedly this rhythm becomes the form called *renga* ("linked verse"), which thrived as a poetic form in the late medieval period. Military leaders on campaigns, gathering to drink *sake* between battles, enjoyed composing refined *renga*. In these *renga* the first phrase became especially important, and was given the name *hokku*. This *hokku* then gained independence as a separate poetic form, which came to be called *haiku*.

The poet who established *haiku* as a definite poetic form, and elevated it to esthetic heights, was Matsuo Bashô (1644—1694). Bashô's art reached its perfection at the beginning of the *Genroku* era. The brief *Genroku* period (1688—1703), coming about one hundred years after the long wars that ended the medieval period, saw the full blossoming of Edo culture.

Bashô loved traveling; he lived to travel, and he died on a journey. We still have five of his travel diaries. The last of these, *Oku no Hosomichi* (literally, "The Narrow Inland Roads," often called "Journey to the North") contains notes and *haiku* from his trip to the northeastern region in 1689. It is his best known and most representative work.

> Spring goes quickly
> A bird cries, and tears are found

In the fish's eye.

This *haiku* gives Bashô's thoughts as he was leaving Edo on a trip. By that time Bashô's name was well-known, and even in rural frontiers like the northeast, people of learning would wait to ask instruction from him. They were usually village leaders, or wealthy merchants, "on-the-spot disciples" of Bashô at whose houses he would stay awhile, and then continue on his journey.

On a stormy sea,
Crossing to Sado is the
River of heaven.

Bashô wrote this *haiku* as he looked at Sado Island while on a journey along the Japan Sea coast.

In 1694, while visiting a disciple in Osaka, Bashô suddenly became ill. He died, leaving the following verse:

Sick on a journey,
My dream is of wintry fields,
Around which I walk.

The basic esthetic principles that underlie Bashô's *haiku* cannot be expressed simply, but they are often referred to as *sabi, wabi*, and *karumi*. These terms reflected, on one side, the urban society of the times, while at the same time there was a continuation of the medieval tradition of *yûgen*.

Sabi comes from the word *sabishi* (lonely). According to Dr. Hisamatsu Sen'ichi, in *The Vocabulary of Japanese Literary Aesthetics*, *sabi* is close to the sense of solitude, as well as of "loneliness in splendor," or "isolation in grandeur." The same scholar sees *wabi* as derived from the verb *wabu* (to be lonely), but while *sabishi* is used in connection with the emotions, *wabu* is used more frequently to refer to living conditions. *Sabi* and *wabi* are mutually related as esthetic concepts, but they differ in that *sabi* is used of beauty in literature and *wabi* in connection with beauty in ordinary life. As an example of this use of *wabi*, one can cite the term, *wabi-cha*, used to express the spirit of the tea ceremony, meaning the attitude of trying to see beauty in the ordinary things of life.

Karumi is the noun form of the adjective *karui* (or *karushi*), meaning "light", "not heavy." This term is repeatedly used by Bashô in his essays on poetry. His *karumi* refers to a combination of simplicity of style and subtleness of content. In this sense *karumi* seems close to the medieval notion of quiet, refined beauty.

About one hundred years after Bashô's death, Yosa Buson gave *haiku* a fresh style. His *haiku* are highly impressive as they give us very vivid images of what he describes in his *haiku*. The following is his best-known *haiku*:

> Yellow rape blossoms —
> In the East rises the moon;
> West, the sun lingers.

Finally toward the end of the Edo period, Kobayashi Issa wrote warm-hearted, gentle *haiku* about human feelings.

Popular Novels

The representative novelist of the early Edo period was Ihara Saikaku (1642-1693). Takizawa Bakin (1767-1848) was representative of late Edo.

As has been pointed out above, the Edo period was a time when merchants flourished. In time this gave birth to a new class of readers of novels. Saikaku himself was born into an Osaka merchant family. He responded to the demands of the times more than did the *haiku* poets, writing many novels which told stories of love and lust, of city dwellers, and of *bushi* as well. Since his style pointedly and honestly depicted the facts—the real character of human lust and greed—he is often compared to Balzac. His stories about city dwellers, the people who said, "In this world, money is almighty," reflect well the life of the prosperous merchants of the period.

Takizawa Bakin was born of a *bushi* family, but later he lived the life of a writer, and wrote many novels. His best work, *Satomi Hakken-den*, was written late in life, and it took him twenty-eight years to complete it. It tells the story of the eight heroes of the Satomi clan. Bakin was a popular novelist, and since his books were printed with wooden plates, many copies were made. It is interesting that the occupation of novelist was established as early as this period.

However, in spite of being the most popular writer of the time, he lived in poverty. For, despite pressure from his publisher for more popular, more entertaining novels, he devoted himself to writing *Satomi Hakken-den* from his forty-seventh year. He lost his eyesight through working too hard on his life work; yet he continued writing this great novel by dictating it to his daughter.

In this period humorous stories catering to the tastes of the masses also were very popular. The best example of these writers is Jippen-sha Ikku. The heroes of his stories, Yaji-san and Kita-san, even now represent a funny duo (like the Americans Abbot and Costello).

Bunraku and *Kabuki*

The most popular forms of theater among the masses in the Edo period were *bunraku* and *kabuki*. *Bunraku* is an artistic union of narration, music, and puppets. The narration and music together are known as *jôruri*. The best-known writer is Chikamatsu Monzayemon, who also wrote plays for *kabuki*. In his beautiful and brilliant scripts he catches those things that move deep in the human heart.

Because of such plays as *Sonezaki Shinjû* (*The Love Suicides at Sonezaki*), *Meido no Hikyaku* (*The Courier for Hell*), *Shinjû Ten no Amijima* (*The Love Suicides at Amijima*), among many other works, he is sometimes called the "Shakespeare of Japan". Many of his works are stories of double suicides, reflecting both the severity of the restrictions of feudal society, and Japanese views of life and death. The Japanese have a disposition to ask not only, "How shall I live?" but even more seriously, "How shall I die?" If ordinary men and women, prevented from marrying by family status or other conditions, sought to be united in the next world by dying together, other people could sympathize with them and grieve for them, and see their stories as beautiful.

This glorification of death, especially what might be called an ethical sense of the glory of suicide, is probably hard for the Western reader to understand, because of the influence on Western culture of the traditional Christian teaching that suicide is wrong. But in the climate of Japanese culture, the hedge that grows to separate life and death is very low. It follows that suicide is one of the permissible choices in life. Moreover, since the purity of spirit involved can be exhibited through tragic drama, suicide became a theme for literature.

Bunraku puppet theater thrived in the early Edo period, but in time was largely supplemented by *kabuki*. *Kabuki*, an exceedingly stylized theater, became very popular among the populace at large in the latter half of the Edo period. In the cities it was performed regularly, and even villages had *kabuki* at festivals. Farmers were fond of performing *kabuki*.

The most famous *kabuki* playwright of the period was Kawatake Mokuami (1816-1893), who wrote more than three hundred sixty original plays, and whose plays are still frequently performed. In addition, he revised and completed other scripts left by previous writers.

V   Modern Literature

The Beginnings of the Modern Novel

The modern period in Japan began with the Meiji period (1868-1912). The feudalistic Tokugawa *bakufu*, which had lasted for so long, finally collapsed and was quickly cast off so that a new Japan could emerge. The shock which brought this change was, of course, the encounter with Western civilization and Western military power.

When the Japanese of that time surveyed the developed Western culture (after 250 years of almost complete isolation), they were enthralled. The Japanese leadership aimed at making Japan Western. Japanese tradition seemed antique — and as antique, bad — thus something to be forgotten, discarded.

At about this time a German physician, E. von Bälz, visited Japan. In his diary he made the following report of what Japanese intellectuals said: "Japan has no history. Japanese history starts from now."

Such a statement was not exceptional; most educated people of that time really believed it. If something was Western, it was always regarded as good. Western machinery, of course, but also Western learning, thought, systems, and customs of food, dress and abode were admired and adopted; at least efforts were made to adopt them. However, such simple imitation was not rearing a new culture. The first twenty years of Meiji, when Japan was breathlessly catching up with Western civilization, was, in the world of literature, on the whole a period of confusion and lifeless stagnation.

In 1887, Futabatei Shimei wrote the novel *Ukigumo* (*The Drifting Cloud*). It marks the beginning of modern Japanese literature. Although *Ukigumo* was not an outstanding novel, it had great significance in using everyday speech, and dealing with people's ordinary life and its difficulties. Futabatei studied, and then took as his model, the contemporary Russian novels.

When Mori Ôgai (1862-1922) returned from study in Germany, he began to introduce European literary theories to Japan. He used his strength in languages to make outstanding Japanese translations of Western novels and plays. His work proved a remarkable stimulus to modern Japanese literature.

From that time, signs of a gradual revival of the literary arts in Japan could be seen. Ozaki Kôyô and Kôda Rohan were representative novelists who flourished during this period. However, the first true genius in modern literature in the early Meiji period, who is still widely read and given high critical acclaim beyond her significance in literary history, is a woman writer Higuchi Ichiyô (1872-1896).

She died at the age of twenty-four, leaving only a little over ten stories and a diary. Though she wrote in the language of an earlier period, her stories are acutely close to the truth about human beings, so that they are strikingly contemporary. Thus they probably have lasting value.

Mori Ôgai, the leading critic of that time, in his famous comment on most contemporary writers, remarked, "It would do contemporary authors good to take a little of her fingernail dirt as medicine."

For a long time the world of *haiku* was stagnant, too, needing an outstanding new figure who would breathe new spirit into it.

Masaoka Shiki (1867-1902) filled this need, and even today *haiku* styles are under his influence.

There was a transformation in *tanka* as well, brought about mainly by Yosano Tekkan, whose wife Akiko surpassed him as an outstanding poet. Tekkan started the journal *Myôjô* ("Morning Star"), which became a vehicle for new, fresh Japanese poets. Ishikawa Takuboku (1886-1912) was a member of that group.

Late Meiji Writers

Toward the end of the Meiji period, one by one real novelists appeared. Shimazaki Tôson (1872-1943), Tayama Katai, Masamune Hakuchô, and Tokuda Shûsei, all of whom wrote many novels with the goal of depicting human existence as it is. They are usually called "naturalists", but they differ considerably from the European naturalists.

The Japanese naturalists aimed at writing only about life as it is. Despising fiction, their writing gradually moved close either to autobiographical narratives or the Japanese traditional miscellanies. Their writing lacked structure and fictional interest. However this criticism should not be taken to disparage their writings; for in Japan there is a long tradition of including non-fiction as well as fiction in the category of "novel."

Of course, there were different schools as well. Nagai Kafû (1879-1959) studied in America and France, and wrote serious novels based on his experiences; *Stories from America*, and *Stories from France*. But after the "Kôtoku high treason affair," despairing of Japanese society, his style changed completely. The "Kôtoku affair" was an incident in which after an attempt to assassinate the Emperor, socialists were arrested along with those who made the bomb, were unjustly convicted, and executed.

Feeling the shock of the incident, Ishikawa Takuboku wrote the poem *One Spoon of Cocoa*, which begins as follows: "I know the sorrowing hearts of the terrorists . . ." Takuboku wrote poems with deep sympathy for the desperate anguish of those who went so far as to attack the Emperor with homemade bombs, in their resistance against this "time of winter" when freedom of thought and opinion was suppressed. On the other hand, Kafû did as the Edo period writers had done — he resolved to turn his back on all politics and devote his attention, and writing, entirely to "decadent" beauty.

Kafû is sometimes linked with Tanizaki Jun'ichirô (1886-1965). These two writers can perhaps be said to have devoted themselves solely to the pursuit of the beautiful.

As has been indicated above, Mori Ôgai did a great deal of work as a critic and mediator for Western literature. Among Japanese he is also very highly esteemed as a novelist, especially for his books that took historical events for their subject matter. But since his novels are, so to speak, austere (*shibui*), it is difficult to find many zealous admirers among Western readers.

Natsume Sôseki, who wrote his first novel, *Wagahai wa Neko de Aru* (*I Am a Cat*) at the urging of Masaoka Shiki, was a humorous novelist at first. *Botchan* still has the most readers of any novel in Japan. Many Japanese read this novel first in their middle-school days. *Botchan* can be said to be a kind of required introduction to the novel for Japanese, perhaps accounting for its popularity. Other representative works of Sôseki are *Sanshirô, Sorekara* (*And Then . . .*), *Mon* (*Gate*), and *Kokoro* (*The Heart*).

Taishô Period Authors

According to Japanese custom, when there is a change in Emperors, the era name changes as well. Following this custom, I would like to treat the Taishô period as a unit in the development of Japanese literature.

The transition from Meiji to Taishô was reflected by the new literary movement built around the journal, *Shirakaba* ("White Birch"). The leader of the "Shirakaba Group," as they were called, was Mushanokôji Sane'atsu. Other principal members were Shiga Naoya, Arishima Takeo, Satomi Ton, and Nagayo Yoshio. Stated extremely briefly, the "Shirakaba Group" was a group of humanists drawn mostly from upper-class families. One marked feature was their long lives.

Arishima was an exception, dying young. From his youth he was deeply concerned about social problems, and he gave up his own farm to his tenants. In the *Descendants of Cain*, he left an excellent novel. In 1923, however, he committed suicide together with a beautiful married woman he loved.

Perhaps one can say that the work of Akutagawa Ryûnosuke is representative of Taishô period literature — witty, slightly sarcastic short stories. He was an unusually able storyteller — a craftsman. Ryûnosuke borrowed the raw material for some of his most famous stories from the *Konjaku Monogatari*, for example, *Hana* (*The Nose*). In 1927 he ended his own life, giving as the reason for his suicide in a note he left behind, "a vague anxiety." His writings in the few years preceding his death had shown a kind of grim intensity of feeling.

Early Shôwa Period Writers

Again there was a change of Emperor, and from 1926 to the present is called the Shôwa era. Early in this period new writers appeared, in several stylistic schools. The works of three women writers, Miyamoto Yuriko, Hirabayashi Taiko, and Sata Ineko can be taken as typical of the period's "proletarian" literature. But there was also a group which insisted on art — only art. This movement created by Yokomitsu Riichi and others was called the "*Shin-kankaku-ha*" ("new sensibility school"). An example of one of its works of continuing interest is Kawabata Yasunari's *Izu no Odoriko* (*The Izu Dancer*).

However, veterans of the Taishô period also continued to be active in this era. Shimazaki Tôson wrote his great work *Yoakemaye* (*Before the Dawn*). Tanizaki Jun'ichirô and Nagai Kafû as well wrote their best novels in this period.

While the Taishô period was one of peace, war came during Shôwa. As the power of militarism grew stronger, literature continued to flow, but only as a thin stream. In the middle of the darkness as Japan headed toward war, new writers began to emerge: Ibuse Masuji, Nakajima Atsushi, Ozaki Kazuo, and Dazai Osamu, among others.

After the war with China began, the military sent many writers to the battlefront, and a lot of reports were written; but considered as literature, they were not well written. There was, however, one exception, a best-seller of the time, Hino Ashihei's *Mugi to Heitai* (*Wheat Fields and Soldiers*).

Literature of the Post-Second World War Period

When the war ended, it seemed that every flower in literature tried to bloom at the same time. During the war Nagai Kafû and Tanizaki Jun'ichirô had continued their work, secretly and laboriously, and these works were published in rapid succession. Similarly, Kawabata Yasunari wrote his famous books, *Thousand Cranes* and *The Sound of the Mountain*. Dazai Osamu, Ishikawa Jun, Sakaguchi Ango and others, delivering what might be called a "body blow," portrayed the joys and sorrows of confused Japanese post-war society.

With the end of war and the advent of peace, new writers gradually appeared. Noma Hiroshi, Umezaki Haruo, Shiina Rinzô, Ôoka Shôhei (b. 1909), Mishima Yukio (1925-1970), Takeda Taijun, Shimao Toshio, and others — all of them, having survived the war, provided a rich group of new writers. In *Sakurajima* (*Cherry Island*), Umezaki pictures the everyday life of a garrison not involved in battle, being stationed in a southern islet of Japan just before Japan's defeat, vividly describing the grudges and bitterness people can entertain. Ôoka, in *Furyo-ki* (*Prisoner of War*), catches with startling clarity of perception his experience and psychic condition as a soldier — starving, exhausted, and finally captured by the enemy. In *Nobi* (*Fires on the Plain*) he portrays the state of mind of an isolated soldier, during a rout on a battlefield in the Philippines, and exhibited skill that is of international level.

In sharp contrast, the war had no direct connection with Mishima Yukio's life during his youth. In *Confessions of a Mask* he relates an honest confession of his own homosexual tendencies, in a way that shocked many people. *The Temple of the Golden Pavilion* is his finest work.

As the confused, rough society calmed down gradually, a group of writers set out to deal in much finer detail with the psychology of everyday life. Among them were Yasuoka Shôtarô and Yoshiyuki Junnosuke (b. 1924). Agawa Hiroyuki described the psychology of youthful enthusiasm with which his generation participated in the *Kamikaze* forces during the war. Yet another contemporary, Endô Shûsaku (b. 1923), writing about the problem of human evil from the viewpoint of the Catholic faith, was introduced to the Western world through translation early in his career.

In the succeeding generation of novelists, Kaikô Takeshi (b. 1930), Ôye Kenzaburô, and in the field of popular literature, Itsuki Hiroyuki, deserve attention.

Japanese Literature Overseas

Since the Meiji period, Japanese literary figures have thought that Japanese literature should be brought to the level of European and American literature, and they have worked to that end. What has been the result? Higuchi Ichiyô, Natsume Sôseki, Tanizaki Jun'ichiro, Kawabata Yasunari, and others, have already attained outstanding international reputations. Among post-war writers, Ôoka Shôhei, Mishima Yukio, Noma Hiroshi, Abe Kôbô, Endô Shûsaku, and more, have been translated into various other languages and found appreciative readers all over the globe.

While introduction to other countries is not necessarily proof of the excellence of a work, for a long time modern Japan was engaged in importing foreign literature. Now, in the last few years, a great deal of Japanese literature is being exported. Japanese literature is gradually receiving marks of recognition in the rest of the world.

Especially in the case of Kawabata, whose literature is thought to be extremely "Japanese," the award of the Nobel Prize pointed up a happy possibility — that of Japanese literature being understood, enjoyed and appreciated abroad — if it is excellent literature. After all, the literary tradition that was born in Japan with the *Kojiki* and the *Mannyôshû*, and continued in the Heian period with the world's oldest and one of its finest novels, the *Genji Monogatari*, still lives. The Meiji intellectuals who said that Japan has no history were wrong. Japanese had been blinded by the splendor of Europe and failed to see the history — including the literary history — which they had inherited themselves.

Forty Essays

Kojiki—

Literature as a Political Prop

Donald L. Philippi

Paradoxically, study of the *Kojiki*, the oldest book in the Japanese language, did not lead me to a study of the other monuments of Japanese literature following it in subsequent centuries. On the contrary, the *Kojiki* awakened in me an interest in the world of oral narrative and song of pre-literature societies, and this interest has since taken me away from Japanese literature as a whole.

The *Kojiki* is an extraordinarily complex work, and those who regard it as merely "history" (or simply as "literature") have certainly failed to grasp its essence. Although it is true that the text of the *Kojiki* resulted from an early attempt at historiography (the more canonical result of which was the *Nihon Shoki* [*Chronicles of Japan*]), analysis of the contents reveals a number of disparate strands, all interwoven to make up a consistent narrative, but nevertheless clearly displaying their essentially different origins.

The mythology in the First Book is especially interesting, since it consists so obviously of two separate myth worlds—the official myth cycle of the Yamato ruling circles (the Takama-no-Hara Myths) and the Izumo myth sequence. The latter cycle is apparently older and is connected with a pantheon of chthonic deities (*kuni-tsu-kami*), the central deity being Ô-kuni-nushi. The conflict between the two myth worlds, and their subsequent conciliation in the land-ceding myth, seems to reflect in a fantastic manner a long process of cultural readjustments and cleavages in early Japan following the introduction of the rice-planting culture, with its Heavenly Deity (*ama-tsu-kami*) religion, its metal implements, and its agricultural ritualism, into an area where the archaic Stone Age cult of chthonic deities had been the religion. The myth figures of the older religion were incorporated into the national pantheon, in which the foremost roles were assigned to the Takama-no-Hara deities. This laid the ideological groundwork for a unified national mythology in which the claims of political and cultural supremacy of the Yamato rulers would be proclaimed, while at the same time certain concessions would be made to the older religious strata. The resulting account, rather than being a consistent mythological tale, is more like a mosaic of various bits and pieces which have been fitted together at a later date for a definite purpose.

The heavenly descent myth, which is the central point of the entire *Kojiki* mythology, is not only a prop for the political claims of the Yamato rulers, who appealed to it to justify their divine rights to rule; it is also the basis for a far-reaching ideology which derives the ancestry of the entire carly Japanese aristocracy from common heavenly forebears. Viewed as statements of the life ideals of the Yamato nobility, the mythological and historical narratives of the *Kojiki* provide us with a wealth of data basic to any study of the origins of Japanese civilization. It is only in this sense that the *Kojiki* is "history."

If we move forward in time, the *Kojiki* is logically connected with many, perhaps even all, of the genres of Japanese literature which were to develop later. We find in the *Kojiki* many songs, tales, and historical anecdotes; there are even embryonic song-dramas. However, the narratives and songs all show signs of a later redaction and are certainly not given to us in their "primitive" form. Thus, in the pages of the *Kojiki* we can only find dim glimpses of the world of oral narrative and song of pre-literate Japan. If we wish to move backward in time into the Stone Age, we must take our leave of the *Kojiki* and turn instead to the oral traditions of the archaic peoples of Northern Asia. For this reason, my interest in the *Kojiki* led me, not to the *Mannyôshû* or the *Genji Monogatari*, but instead to the heroic and mythic epics of the Ainu, who apparently have preserved, in a form relatively free from contamination, the pre-agricultural thought patterns and oral traditions of the archaic hunting and fishing peoples of Northern Asia. Into this world the *Kojiki* gives us only second-hand glimpses.

[Note] *Kojiki* (*Records of Ancient Matters*) is the oldest written document in Japan that has survived till the present. It was initiated by the Emperor Tenmu (?-686) and completed in 712, after his death. The work begins with myths about the creation of the world and the origins of Japan, and gradually moves on to historical events, but it is difficult to distinguish myth from fact. Throughout the *Kojiki* there is a consistent effort to establish the legitimate authority of the imperial line, but the document also clearly includes legends handed down among the people and recollections of historical events.

This work is important from a literary point of view in that it is the oldest book written in Japanese and it contains many ancient myths, stories and poems.

Mannyôshu—

Poems from All Walks of Life of Early Japan

Wolfram Naumann

The *Mannyôshû*, the oldest and the most varied of Japanese lyrical anthologies, dates from the 8th century and shows in its very arrangement the conflict we so often see in Japanese culture. To be sure it contains, especially in the archaic periods, poetry of unmistakably native character in rhythm and theme. But in writing down this material the foreign Chinese characters were used. They were adapted in such an ingenious and creative way that the resulting text was unintelligible to Chinese. It was an irony of fate that the Japanese themselves, two centuries after the compilation of the anthology, had to select an erudite board of scholars to decipher this curious text. Similar dislocations are to be met with in the attempt to classify poetry according to Chinese categories. The terms used for the purpose often bear little or no relationship to the poems designated. In this respect the *Mannyôshû* is a particularly striking example of the consequences of intellectual borrowing.

In comparison with these external difficulties the internal ones are less precise. The contents range from early "vital" topics to later contemplative lyrics clearly showing Chinese or Buddhist influence. Poets and personae come from the widest variety of social backgrounds, from peasant to emperor. Polarity of this nature has made the history of *Mannyôshû* criticism one of prejudice. Some scholars— especially since World War II—have emphasized sociological aspects, with a certain partiality towards the lower classes, drawing heavily on "beggars' songs," the exact meaning or function of which expression is still under dispute. Other critics—they were already prominent in the middle ages and have been even more influential during and since the Meiji era—laid stress upon pathetically expressed loyalty to the Emperor and praised such poets as Kakinomoto no Hitomaro. In the person of this recognized poet laureate who sang the glory of deities, sovereign, and realm, they found the ideal of "sincere devotion to the Emperor." So strong was their conviction of the greatness of Hitomaro and his age that they even saw the influence of prayers the standardized forms of which are noticeably fabricated, which cannot possibly predate the eighth century. The heavily ornamented style of the Shinto ritual (*Norito*) is said to have influenced the vocabulary of Hitomaro, who flourished about 700. Titles are mentioned in earlier documents, to be sure, but the texts themselves were set down in 928. To such a degree did those critics adopt the notion of the superiority of institutionalized norms to the inspiration of the individual that they were unable to conceive of an opposite yet equally justifiable hypothesis: that Hitomaro was the creator (or one of the creators) of this pompous ritualistic style.

In and after the late Heian period Hitomaro, the most famous of *Mannyôshû* poets, was so venerated that incense was offered before his image. We may begin with him to demonstrate the vast range of intellectual and sensual attitudes in the anthology. In an "envoy" to a long anthem upon the Empress Jitô's Yoshino palace, Hitomaro says:

Miredo akanu	Never tired of seeing
Yoshino no kawa no	the River Yoshino
tokoname no	on its smooth rocks
tayuru koto naku	endlessly
mata kaheri mimu　(I, 37)	I shall come again.

Here life is experienced as everlasting and immediate delight. On the other hand the monk Mansei paints in an equally seductive picture the "Endlichkeit" and transience of human existence:

Yo no naka wo	This worldly life,
nani ni tatohemu	what shall I liken it to:
asabiraki	when at the break of day
kogi inishi fune no	a boat is rowed away
ato naki ga goto　(III, 351)	and leaves no trace behind.

A third possibility is the transcendence of the all-too-human craving for the infinite and the Buddhist belief in rebirth. Ôtomo no Tabito ignores both and his humour is such that he treats nothing seriously:

Nakanaka ni		Rather than
hito to arazu wa		be born as man again,
saketsubo ni		a rice-wine jar
nari nite shikamo		I should like to be,
sake ni shiminamu	(III, 343)	soaked with rice-wine!

[Note] *Mannyôshû* literally means a collection of ten thousand leaves, or ten thousand poems, but in fact it is made up of around four thousand five hundred poems. It is the oldest collection of poetry in Japan. The poets whose works are included number about two hundred and sixty, and they come from every social class: from emperors and empresses, aristocrats and court poets to provincial soldiers or farmers and their wives, and even beggars. The poems were composed over a period of about four hundred years, starting in the fourth century, and the date of completion is estimated to be around the middle of the eighth century. As a result, the contents are various: ceremonial poems, banquet poems, love poems, poems related to everyday life, comic poems, lyric poems, etc. The style too varies, but in general a straightforward, unsophisticated, masculine tone of expression is dominant. The poems are written basically in syllable groupings of five and seven, setting the pattern for the *waka* and *haiku* poetry of later generations.

Sangô Shiiki—

A Long Path to Human Freedom

ALLAN G. GRAPARD

This is not an essay, but rather a collection, in diary form, of my impressions of *Sangô Shiiki*, beginning from the time I was first introduced to the work. Within this format, it will be possible, I think, to express in a simplified manner some otherwise complicated ideas.

Paris: April 11, 1968

Today I read an encyclopedia article by Professor Mori Arimasa entitled "The Development of Japanese Buddhism." In his discussion of the growth of Buddhism in Japan, there is a detailed section on Kûkai's *Sangô Shiiki,* a book in which Kûkai evaluates the three major ways of thought in East Asia: Confucianism, Taoism, and Buddhism. This sounds interesting, but there are few books which attempt to compare these three doctrines. Even Japanese scholars have written little on the subject. I shall have to read Kûkai's book, especially if I wish to understand ancient Chinese literature.

Paris: September 1, 1968

I leave for Tokyo next month. Finally, I shall be able to view with my own eyes the cultural phenomena that I have so long admired, and meet the people who have created that culture. If it is true that the Japanese have received their inspiration from the past and from nature, should not I be able to have the same experiences if I go into the mountains and do the same things?

Kyoto: September 13, 1969

I returned to Kyoto yesterday after traveling for four weeks by motorcycle along the route described by Bashô in *The Narrow Inland Roads.* The combination of reading his travelogue and *haiku* and of seeing nature in all its magnificence somehow profoundly moved me.

Kyoto: June 10, 1970

Kûkai and Dôgen are the two pillars in the history of Japanese thought. I must read, study, and translate their works. I obtained a copy of *Sangô Shiiki* this morning. Henceforward I will mainly study this book.

Kyoto: January 20, 1971

Sangô Shiiki is a strange work. It is written in a style common in China in the eighth century. As a young man, Kûkai must have worked extremely hard. However, because he deliberately used very rare Chinese characters, his expressions are stilted; though perhaps it was common in academic circles of that time to show off one's erudition.

I find the theoretical presentation in *Sangô Shiiki* most interesting. The rhythm of its theoretical structure reminds one of the *jo-ha-kyû* (introduction-development-climax) construction of Ze'ami's *noh* drama. The section in which he describes "The Sea of Life and Death" corresponds to the introduction. Next there is the remarkable "Song of Impermanence" with its destructive horrors. The idea of impermanence is an exceedingly important element in Buddhism and a pillar of Japanese culture. Its poetic manifestation in *Sangô Shiiki* corresponds to the development sections of *noh*. The climax appears in "Fruits of Sudden Enlightenment." After the rogues, Confucians and Taoists are all converted to Buddhism, the curtain falls. In the *noh*, slowly and one at a time, the actors leave the stage, cross the passageway, and disappear. The last poem in *Sangô Shiiki* gives exactly the same impression.

Mt. Kôya: March 25, 1971

I could hardly wait to see snow-covered Mt. Kôya, the calligraphy of Kûkai, and the temples.

Kûkai wrote almost nothing about himself. Thus one might think that one can discover his personality only through his writings and biographies about him. Yet a study of his characters, his writing style, and his arrangement of characters on the paper should also give us a glimpse into his mind.

One of the priests at the temple presented me with a photostat of all Kûkai's calligraphy. He is regarded as one of the three greatest calligraphers in Japan.

Kyoto: November 28, 1973

I just finished the French translation of *Sangô Shiiki*. This book is important not merely because it was written by a famous monk, not merely because it was the first example of literature written in Chinese to appear in Japan, not merely because it is at the root of Japanese philosophy, but because it positively proves that there is a path leading to human freedom.   (Tr. by Thomas J. Cogan)

[Note] *Sangô Shiiki* (*Instructions in the Three Teachings*) was written when the author Kûkai was twenty-four years old. In it he comments on which of the three Eastern religions, Confucianism, Taoism, or Buddhism, he considers to be the most profound and most excellent. Kûkai also traces the evolution of his own thought, and the work can be seen as a statement of his own preference for living according to the way of Buddhism.

KÛKAI (774-835) started out as a scholar, but after coming in contact with Buddhism he became completely involved in it, devoting himself to study and asceticism in various places. At the age of thirty-one he went to China, accompanying the Japanese ambassador to the T'ang court. Travelling to Ch'ang-an, the capital city, he studied not only Buddhism, but many different aspects of Chinese culture. On his return to Japan he built a temple on Mount Kôya and founded the *Shingon* sect of Buddhism in Japan. He also exerted great influence on the education of ordinary people, travelling to many areas of the country and giving advice on the development of agriculture. To the average Japanese even today, Kûkai is still one of the best known and most highly respected of all Buddhist monks, known popularly as Kôbô Daishi, or "the Great Teacher Kôbô." He is also famous as a master calligrapher.

Taketori Monogatari—

The Supernatural in Legend and Literature

JACQUES PEZEU

Contemporary Japanese literature is by no means lacking in imaginative works of fiction; several major Japanese writers have become well known in the West thanks to the increasing number of translations. But there is yet another source of the pleasures of the imagination which Japanese literature can offer: the traditional tales, a treasury of poetry and fantasy which is as precious to the Japanese as stories like the Sleeping Beauty are to the French. These tales, often very old, exist in modern versions for both children and educated people. Few of them have as much charm as *Taketori Monogatari* (*The Tale of the Bamboo-Cutter*), a story of an extraordinary child discovered and adopted by an old man and his wife. A little girl of superhuman origin is discovered in a bamboo shoot, brings great wealth to her adopted parents, and is herself destined to live an extraordinary life.

Besides the theme of the child born in a plant, we also find stories of animals who take the form of children and are adopted. But an even more striking theme to Western readers is one that is basic to the story of the bamboo cutter: men who come to court the young princess are rejected one by one when they fail to meet her excessive demands. There are five men of whom the Princess Kaguya, the child found in the bamboo, demands something impossible, such as finding the Buddha's own begging bowl. They all fail, and this is the one notable difference between this story and our Western tales in which the last contender is usually successful, sometimes even with the help of the heroine. After the five suitors comes the Emperor himself, but he is no more successful than the others, and only gains one final advantage over them: the princess reveals to him that she is the daughter of the Moon King and that she must soon return to her home.

This again is a theme familiar to readers of Western tales; Andersen, Grimm, and Perrault have many variations of it, whether the mysterious country in question be at the bottom of the sea, in the sky, or some enchanted kingdom. One is also reminded of the chivalrous tales of the Middle Ages in the West, and all the stories of enchantment related by Don Quixote. However the Princess Kaguya is profoundly different from our legendary princesses. They are tender and lonely young creatures, ready to respond to the love of a handsome and wealthy young man, while Princess Kaguya strikes us as being cold and unfeeling. She deliberately proposes impossible tasks to all her suitors, while the Western fairy tale princess helps at least one among them, the one to whom she has given her heart.

In the Western tradition, a mysterious young girl, even if she has come from heaven, dreams only of becoming united with a mortal. Kaguya, on the other hand, cannot fall in love with a human being, feeling no joy until the day when she will fly away again to her distant homeland. Could this be a reflection of Japanese pessimism? Man's destiny is a miserable one and is not attractive to a woman from another world. Furthermore, the princess is not sufficiently attached to any man to suggest bringing him back with her to her marvelous kingdom. There is then an invisible but unbridgeable gap between humans and beings from the superhuman world; their relationships are never definitive, nor can they ever enter each other's worlds. This is an element completely foreign to our Western tales where the young lady from extra-terrestrial regions generally agrees to become a mortal for the sake of love, and renounces her higher destiny. Could it be that love in Japan is not strong enough for that? Or is it that love is not universal and the mysterious creatures from another world cannot experience it? In any case, with their intense poetry and exoticism mixed with familiar images, the old Japanese tales make up one of the oldest and most attractive aspects of the literature of Japan.   (Tr. by William Currie)

[Note] *Taketori Monogatari* (*The Tale of the Bamboo-Cutter*) is said to have been written at the beginning of the tenth century or perhaps even before that. Murasaki Shikibu, the authoress of *The Tale of Genji*, called this story the "oldest ancestor of prose tales." Since it is the story of Princess Kaguya, the heroine discovered in a bamboo joint by an old man who goes out to collect bamboo, it also has the title *Princess Kaguya*. When she grows up to be a beauty, suitors appear one after another, but she lays down what seem to be impossible conditions, and the young men all fail. Then on the evening of the full moon of August fifteenth, she returns to the kingdom of the moon.

This tale has been skillfully put together and made into one single story from Indian Buddhist scriptures, Chinese legends, and stories handed down from long ago in Japan.

Makura no Sôshi—

Sei Shônagon and her Pillow Book

IVAN MORRIS

She was born about 965 and served as lady-in-waiting to Empress Teishi during the last decade of the tenth century. Her father was Motosuke, a member of the Kiyowara family, who worked as a provincial official but was best known as a scholar and a poet. It is possible that Shônagon was briefly married to a government official called Tachibana no Norimitsu, by whom she may have had a son, but so vague is our knowledge about her life that even this is uncertain. Uncertain too is the tradition that she died in lonely poverty. We are not even sure of her real name. In the palace she was called Shônagon (Minor Counsellor), but recent research suggests that her name may actually have been Nagiko; Sei refers to the Kiyowara family.

In a section of *The Pillow Book* that can be dated about 994 Shônagon writes:

One day Lord Korechika, the Minister of the Centre, brought the Empress a bundle of notebooks. "What shall we do with them?" Her Majesty asked me . . .

"Let me make them into a pillow," I said.

"Very well," said Her Majesty. "You may have them."

Now I had a vast quantity of paper at my disposal, and I set about filling the notebooks with odd facts, stories from the past, and all sorts of other things, often including the most trivial material. On the whole I concentrated on things and people that I found charming and splendid; my notes are also full of poems and observations about trees and plants, birds and insects.

Shônagon started work on her famous book while still serving in the Court whose life she describes with such minute detail. Some of the sections, however, were written many years later than the events they record, and the work was not completed until well after Shô-nagon's retirement following the Empress's death in 1000.

Though this is the one and only collection of its type to have survived from the Heian period, it is probable that many others were written. The title, *Makura no Sôshi* ("notes of the pillow"), whether or not Shônagon actually used it herself, was probably a generic term to describe a type of informal book of notes which men and women composed when they retired to their rooms in the evening and which they kept near their sleeping place, possibly in the drawers of their wooden pillows, so that they might record stray impressions. *The Pillow Book* was the precursor of the typically Japanese genre known as *zuihitsu* ("occasional writings," "random notes") which has lasted until the present day and which includes some of the most valued works in the country's literature.

The original text of Shônagon's book had disappeared well before the end of the Heian period, and by the beginning of the military era in the twelfth century numerous variants were already in circulation. We shall probably never know which is the closest to the original. Much depends on whether Shônagon was, as she states in the book, writing only for herself, or whether she had other readers in mind. It is possible that *The Pillow Book* was begun casually as a sort of private notebook-diary, and that only after its existence became known at Court did it develop into a more deliberate and literary work. In this case Shônagon may herself have rearranged some of the sections of her book in order to make it more coherent and readable.

The structural confusion of *The Pillow Book* is often regarded as its main stylistic weakness. Yet surely part of the book's charm lies precisely in its rather bizarre, haphazard arrangement in which a list of "awkward things," for example, is followed by an account of the Emperor's return from a shrine, after which comes a totally unrelated incident about the Chancellor that occurred a year or two earlier and then a short, lyrical description of the dew on a clear autumn morning.

[Note] *Makura no Sôshi* (*The Pillow Book*) ranks with *The Tale of Genji* as an outstanding example of the literature written by women during the Heian period. As opposed to *Genji*, which is a novel with a full-scale plot, *The Pillow Book* is the first example of a traditional genre in Japanese literature: a unique sort of essay collection called *zuihitsu*, literally "following the brush." Compared with *Genji*, which is filled with a deeply felt artistic effect, the style of *The Pillow Book* is lively, impressing the reader with its flashes of sharp wit.

The authoress, SEI SHÔNAGON (ca.965~ca.1020) came from an aristocratic family of scholars. After an unhappy marriage she served at court at about the same time as Murasaki Shikibu, winning the favor of the Empress because of her literary ability.

Genji Monogatari—

How Many People Wrote The Tale of Genji ?

EDWARD G. SEIDENSTICKER

"The problem is whether they are by him or by someone else of the same name," said someone facetiously of the Baconian theory. Whoever wrote *The Tale of Genji* was wise enough to remain nameless, and so there is no problem. No one doubts that it is one of the finest products of the high Heian Period, and that it is by — and here the wisdom of the Japanese language would interpose itself to dismiss another problem by not requiring that we choose between the singular and the plural. "By a lady," I was about to say, and to add that she might as well be called Murasaki Shikibu as anything else. But should it be the singular or the plural? The theory of dual or even multiple authorship is in *Genji* studies the equivalent of the Baconian theory.

The Tale of Genji obviously breaks into two parts with the sudden announcement in the first sentence of the forty-second chapter that Genji is dead. The second part begins very tentatively and awkwardly with stories, occupying three chapters, that come to nothing. Almost every reader feels a certain loss of control, an insecurity, a want of direction, and it is very easy to conclude that one writer has departed the scene and a less confident writer taken over.

From the forty-fifth chapter the action departs the city and we have the story of a younger generation, Genji's nieces and grandson and the grandson of his best friend. The precise scholarly evidence supporting or refuting the *Genji* Baconians is and probably always will be inconclusive, though the computers would not yet seem to have had their say. What matters most is one's reading of the last ten chapters. Do they, as the three transitional chapters unquestionably do, suggest insecurity and irresolution, or do they give evidence of as firm a hand as the earlier chapters? If the former, then the debate between single and dual authorship comes to something not much different from a flip of a coin. If the latter, then the argument for dual authorship seems to require a miracle within a miracle, and that is beyond the powers of most of us to imagine. It is a miracle that the *Genji* came to be at all, since so little in either Chinese or Japanese literature foreshadows it. For two masterpieces to appear in quick succession (we know that upwards of fifty chapters were in existence by about 1020), with nothing to foreshadow them and nothing to succeed them — so compounds the miracle as to put it beyond the imaginative grasp of most of us.

It becomes, then, a matter of the reader's impressions. I shall offer mine after I have offered those of another *Genji* translator, Mrs. Enchi Fumiko, who recently finished putting it into modern Japanese. Until she translated them herself, she said recently, she thought the last ten chapters the best part of the *Genji*. Now she detects differences in style from the earlier chapters, and feels that even as there is a diminution in the action, which moves from the center of things, the court, to the periphery, so too there seems to be a narrowing of the author's vision. She also detects the presence of a late-Heian sensibility. Tentatively, then, she seems to have become a *Genji* Baconian.

My own view is that, though there are occasional lapses, as in the three transitional chapters, the *Genji* gets better as it proceeds. The diminution in the action is accompanied by greater intensity of vision. One can see the author of the first chapters growing older and wiser. The problem of the order in which the first chapters were written is very complicated, but the point of departure would seem to be the tenth century romance with its idealized hero and its often improbable and sentimental events. From about a third of the way through the vast narrative, the hero becomes more recognizably human and the portrait of him is increasingly somber and presently somewhat tragic. Then with his disappearance the author seems to lose interest in realism and the characterization becomes more abstract. This is not to say that it becomes less interesting. On the contrary, as the characters diminish in human stature, and undeniably they do, they take on a certain abstract, symbolic significance as representatives of us all in the confrontation with fate.

So my answer is the opposite to Mrs. Enchi's. Perhaps when everyone has taken sides we will have something like a final answer and will not need to consult the computers. Even those who hold for single authorship may find certain passages suspicious. The question to be asked about the three suspect chapters following Genji's death is: who could have wished to write them? The answer may suggest that at least one of them, "Bamboo River," the forty-fourth, is spurious.

[Note] *Genji Monogatari* (*The Tale of Genji*) is known as the world's first full-length novel. The date of its composition is estimated to be at the beginning of the eleventh century. This work is the great masterpiece of classical Japanese literature.

The first forty-one chapters are set against the brilliant background of the Heian court, depicting the life of the surpassingly handsome and accomplished Hikaru Genji, the shining prince. This part of the book explores his numerous love affairs and unprecedented successes, but it also records the subsequent unhappy events in his life and his troubled last years following his fall from glory. The last thirteen chapters of the novel present an entirely different atmosphere. Genji's son becomes the central character, and the prominent theme is the conflict between human passion and the search for truth.

The authoress, MURASAKI SHIKIBU (ca.978~ca.1014), a member of the powerful Fujiwara clan, served at court after her husband's death. A diary which she wrote is also extant.

Konjaku Monogatari—

Folk Tales with Emotional Realism

DOUGLAS E. MILLS

To begin this invitation to read *Konjaku Monogatari* on a negative note may seem curious, but it would be wrong to gloss over the limitations of the work; fascinating though it is, as literature it is not to be mentioned in the same breath as a *Genji Monogatari*. The stories have none of the latter's subtle psychological insights, being told entirely in terms of events; though they are enlivened by many skillful touches, the narrative technique is in general simple and direct to the point of naïveté: the language is plain and often prolix, without the literary refinement and allusive economy of court literature. The elegance of *mono no aware* and the Heian preoccupation with man's emotional reaction to nature is totally lacking; and the keynote is rather one of didacticism, often quite trite and tiresome. It is not altogether surprising, then, that early modern scholars of Japanese literature like Haga (in the beginning at least) and Fujioka regarded the work as of no value as literature, but only as a source (it is in fact a veritable treasure house) of information for the student of folklore, superstition, popular religion, and manners and customs.

The recognition that this judgment is unjust dates largely from the praise given to *Konjaku* by the great short story writer Akutagawa (1892-1927). Later the pendulum swung even further, with impassioned advocacy of the literary merit of the collection by one or two super-enthusiasts. The truth surely lies some way short of their claims. In particular, it seems wrong to talk of tales which, while in no sense folk literature, cannot without reserve be treated as original creations in terms more appropriate to the criticism of twentieth-century fiction.

Despite these reservations, however, we are left with the undoubted fact that this vast compilation of stories, Buddhist and secular, foreign and native, derived both from written sources and from oral tradition, has immense human appeal. It has been aptly described as "a mirror of ancient Japan." It is no compilation of fairy stories or tales of never-never-land. Exactly why this collection of Buddhist miracle-tales and other homilies accompanied by secular tales of astonishing diversity (including some that are highly earthy, not to say unedifying) was ever compiled, and by what person or persons, we do not know, though the compilation most probably had some connection with preaching. What can be said is that the attitude throughout holds the events related to have actually happened, and to have been recorded because they were inspiring, frightening, touching, amusing, shocking, or simply intriguing. Thus we read not only of the comforts and wonders of religion but of all manner of happenings in ordinary life. Inevitably, in that superstition-ridden society, the mysterious and the supernatural loom large, and it is certainly that element in the stories which attracted Akutagawa. So too did the element of the grotesque (the pathetic Goi in *Imogayu* [*Yam Gruel*], based on *Konjaku* 26/17, or the desire of Heichû to cure himself of a hopeless love by looking at the contents of his mistress's chamberpot, in *Kôshoku* [*Lust*] based on *Konjaku* 30/1). For Akutagawa *Konjaku* had a freshness and uninhibited vigour which led him to speak of its "beauty of brutality." It is the down-to-earth quality—so different from court romances or poetic diaries—which makes the *Konjaku* picture of society so full and vital. Not all the stories, of course, can be said to bring their characters to life (particularly in the more stereotyped Buddhist sections). But many do, especially the secular tales; here we are reading of real people, we see all ranks of society, high and low, and we see them "warts and all"—young nobles brawling in the street or playing practical jokes, lecherous or impostor priests, "con-men" and tricksters. The world we observe is one in which a man must have his wits about him. In the far from settled transitional period just before and after the year 1100, there was much nostalgia for "the good old days," but there were also conspicuous signs of the changes which led to the world of feudalism. Nowhere can this be seen better than in *Konjaku Monogatari*.

If the general reader is seeking refined aesthetic enjoyment, then *Konjaku* is not for him. But if he wishes an understanding of the ordinary concerns of Heian people, and in particular of the common people whom courtly literature neglected altogether, he cannot do better than sample the unpretentious but often lively stories which for Akutagawa were a sort of "Comédie humaine." He will perhaps share Akutagawa's feeling that every time he opens *Konjaku*, he "seems to hear the people of those days sending up their cries of grief and merriment."

[Note] *Konjaku Monogatari* (*Tales of Ages Ago*) is Japan's largest collection of medieval legends, put together during the twelfth century. The stories number 1065 in all, and are drawn from three separate traditions: Indian, Chinese, and Japanese. They were originally collected as tales illustrative of Buddhist teachings, to be used at Buddhist gatherings. Among the Japanese stories there are some dealing with every class of society, from emperors and aristocrats to priests, warriors, farmers, merchants, thieves and beggars.

Heike Monogatari—

History or Literature ?

JEAN-RENÉ CHOLLEY

One of the main points of interest in the *Heike Monogatari* (*Tales of the Heike*) is without question the depiction of the series of battles that took place during the wars between the Heike clan, then masters of Japan, and the rising Genji house, who were to take control of the country and create a new feudal system. The rapidly declining fortunes of the Heike rulers are set against the ever-growing influence and military power of the surging Genji clan in a point-counterpoint manner, thus providing a general view of the climate of the times and of the thoughts that stirred the minds of the main protagonists of the "coup d'état" that put a final stop to the convulsions that shook the Heian period. The *Heike Monogatari*, being primarily a war tale, is oriented toward action and the immediate causes that set people in motion. The passages describing the battles at Ichi no Tani, Yashima, and Dan no Ura in particular are justly famed for their fine grasp of atmosphere and character (one is reminded of Yoshitsune driving his horse into the sea under the rain of arrows from the Heike side while trying to retrieve his bow, a detail that tells pages about the real Yoshitsune). But even a casual reading impresses the reader with the fact that the *Heike* is singularly lacking in any consideration of the remoter causes of the war, and that it is only concerned with the fate of warriors determined to grab as much power as they could for themselves without thought for the country they were putting through sword and fire. It has been widely remarked, though mainly outside Japan, that the *Heike* lacks historical dimension, especially when compared with the *Taiheiki* (*Record of the Great Peace*), a later work with fewer pretensions to moralization and of much lesser fame. This is not to dispute the fact that a war tale should be essentially concerned with warriors and their fights, but an undue emphasis on purely military processes finally leads to the unpleasant impression that these events constitute a world by themselves, following each other as if they were links in a chain of causes and effects, thus suggesting that the Genji uprising was ultimately a military phenomenon. Given the ideas of the time and the need to escape from the stifling atmosphere of the over-civilized Heian court nobles, this may well have been one of the unconscious aims of the tale. But purely military matters rank very low on the scale of significant historical events; they are more often the catalysts than the causes of important historical changes. The vista offered by the *Heike* might have been more satisfying and its interest greatly enhanced if it had shown the rising Eastern warriors, and particularly Yoritomo, not only as warlords, but also as shrewd opportunists who could size up the waning strength of the power structure centered in Kyoto, and could see that the country was theirs for the picking.

But then it may be unadvisable to look for historical analysis of political or social processes in a literary work, which is what the *Heike* is in the first place. And moreover, the *Heike* is not without a historical sense of its own. The pervading sense of rise and decline in the victories of the Genji and the ultimate defeat and near annihilation of the Heike illustrates the belief that all things are impermanent; and this Buddhist notion of transience lifts the *Heike* to the level of a higher historical view that has only recently been discovered in the West. Political and social systems, cultures and civilizations are mortal, they are as subject to decay and death as the men who make them, and, through the four words that have become a symbol of the *Heike*, *shôja hissui*, "those who rise must fall," one can see the fate of the new Kamakura rulers beyond the victories of the Genji.

[Note] *Heike Monogatari* (*Tales of the Heike*) is the representative masterpiece of the many military chronicles written in the period following the turbulent civil wars of Japan's middle ages. It follows the fortunes of the Heike clan from the height of their power to their eventual defeat by the Genji clan and so the descriptions of battle scenes are particularly numerous. Underlying the entire work is the Buddhist theme of the impermanence of all things, a note which is sounded with the opening paragraph: "Even the mighty must fall. The proud ones too do not last long." These heroic tales are filled with sadness. The whole work was composed in verse and recited by many blind entertainers playing a stringed instrument called the *biwa*. Their audiences listened attentively and shed copious tears. The influence which the work exercised on the sentiments of the Japanese people in succeeding generations was very great.

Tannishô—

Salvation in the Latter Days of the Law

JEAN-NOËL ROBERT

This very short treatise (it fills at most fifty small size printed pages, including philological notes and commentary), written in a simple style understandable even to the modern Japanese of average culture, has come to be most highly regarded in the True Sect of Pure Land (*Jôdo Shin Shû*) of Japanese Buddhism, as well as in other Pure Land Sects, and, by now, has become a part of the common literary knowledge of the Japanese.

The Pure Land doctrines, the origin of which can be traced back to India, were first systematized in China by the great masters T'an-luan (476-542), Tao-chao (562-645), and Shan-tao (613-681). Brought to Japan very early, they came to have independent importance with the rise of Hônen (1133-1212), who founded the Pure Land Sect (*Jôdo Shû*) and emphasized the importance of the Three Great Canonical Texts of Pure Land (*Jôdo Sanbu Kyô: Muryôju Kyô, Kan Muryôju Kyô, Amida Kyô*) together with the teachings of Shan-tao. The most important tenet of Pure Land Buddhism was the belief in the efficacy of the forty-eight original vows made by the Buddha Amida while he was still a bodhisattva, and especially the eighteenth, often called the "Royal Original Vow," by which he vowed never to enter Buddhahood unless every living being who wishes earnestly to be reborn in his Pure Land should be able to do so merely by invoking the name of Amida ten times (*nenbutsu*). This belief was closely connected with the belief that a time had come when the Buddhist Law could no longer be comprehended or practiced (the latter days of the law, *mappô*). Thus man no longer possessed the power to achieve his own liberation (inherent power, *jiriki*); he had to rely upon the superior power of the Buddha Amida (*tariki*, power from without), who could guide him to his Paradise (*gokuraku*

= *jôdo*).

In the school of Hônen, therefore, the invocation of the name of Amida was the principal form of religious practice, though there still lingered the belief in the efficacy of building temples and of the observance of religious discipline (*kairitsu*); moreover, the number of recitations was still regarded as significant.

The True Sect of Pure Land was a reaction against these survivals and a radicalization of the fideist, or rather quietist, aspects of Amidism.

In the *Tannishô* (*The Analects of Shinran*), we have a collection of sayings by the founder of the sect, Shinran (1173-1262), a disciple of Hônen. He first studied Buddhist doctrine at the center of the Tendai sect, one of the oldest and most elaborate sects of Japan, but little satisfied with this sophisticated scholasticism, he left Mt. Hiyei and was converted by Hônen to faith in the vow of Amida. His long life was full of tribulations, but it will suffice to say that his thought and *dicta* are set forth in the doctrinal compendium *Kyôgyô-Shinshô* in six fascicles, and in the *Tannishô*. This last book was not written by Shinran himself, but was edited by his disciple Yuiyen, after his master's death. It contains eighteen "chapters" of a few lines each, with two "prefaces" (*jo*) and one postscript by Yuiyen. It is divided into two parts: the first part, from the beginning to chapter ten, includes the sayings of Shinran as regarded by Yuiyen; the second part, starting from the second preface following chapter ten, consists of the reflections of Yuiyen upon doctrinal divergences and his attempt to correct them by reference to Shinran's *dicta*.

The main characteristics of the doctrine set forth here in fragmentary form are best summed up as fideism: faith (*shin*) in the Original Vow is everything, the only practice necessary is the invocation of Amida with the formula, "*Namu Amida Butsu.*" It is no longer necessary to recite this several thousand times, nor to study sutras or practice discipline — the Difficult Way to salvation (*nandô*). One need only rely upon the power of the Other, which is Amida — this is the Easy Way to salvation (*idô*), open to all, old and young, good and wicked. The most famous chapter of this short book is perhaps the third, where one finds the famous sentence, "If even the good can be reborn in the Pure Land, how much the more so for the wicked!" For the wicked, deprived of the power to gain salvation by themselves are *par excellence* the object of the Great Vow of Amida.

Now, a few words about the literary genre to which the *Tannishô* belongs. It is classified as *hôgo*, literally "a speech on the Law," the equivalent of the Christian sermon. This form developed with the new, more popular Buddhism that arose in the Kamakura period, around the thirteenth century, especially in the Pure Land and Zen sects, but also in the Shingon sect. The *hôgo* were first delivered orally before monks or laymen, and afterwards written down, most often by a disciple rather than by the author himself.

Thus it is that some of the greatest Buddhist works in Japan are *hôgo*, including the *Shôbô Genzô* by Dôgen, numerous works by Nichiren, and of course the *Tannishô*.

[Note] SHINRAN (1173-1262) was a Buddhist monk who at first pursued his studies on Mount Hiyei, and was later engaged in spreading the teachings of Buddha. He founded the True Sect of Pure Land (*Jôdo Shin Shû*), which today has the largest number of followers of any Buddhist sect in Japan. In the turbulent times of war in which he lived, people were looking for peace of soul and were attracted to this new way of faith. The *Tannishô* was written after Shinran's death by his disciple Yuiyen, who deplored the various conflicting views within the same religious sect, and tried to pass on with fidelity the teaching which he had received. The book contains the teachings of Shinran in his last years, and thanks to the enthusiastic style of Yuiyen, it has become a work of literature. The book has also attracted much attention for the way its logic develops, and the following passage is well-known as a point of controversy: "Good people will certainly be saved. Such being the case, how can it be that bad people, by the mercy of Buddha, will not be saved?"

Tsurezuregusa—

The Origins of Japanese Aesthetics

WILLIAM CURRIE

Few works in Japanese literature succeed so well as *Tsurezuregusa* in combining a reflection of the period in which it was written (around 1330) with a flavor that strikes modern readers as quite contemporary. The Buddhist preoccupation with the impermanence of all things which dominated Japanese thought in the middle ages pervades the entire work. At the same time, the author's comments on esthetic ideals and human behavior frequently seem as if they could have been written yesterday. This combination of modernity with traditional esthetics and a traditional Buddhist view of life is perhaps one of the reasons why *Tsurezuregusa* continues to have a strong appeal for a wide audience of readers.

There is no way of measuring the extent to which Yoshida Kenkô, the author of *Tsurezuregusa*, has influenced Japanese manners and esthetics. But it is certain that many generations of Japanese, over hundreds of years, have read this collection of essays and miscellaneous jottings, and so it is possible to speculate that Kenkô has been an important formative influence on many attitudes that are considered "typically Japanese."

The structure of the work itself puts it in that peculiarly Japanese form of literature known as *zuihitsu*, a kind of lyrical essay which literally means "following the brush." Kenkô's style is justly famous, and his influence on later Japanese writing is probably just as important as his influence on esthetic and behavioral ideals in subsequent generations. The two strands of influence are closely connected. It was because of his style that Kenkô's work came to be part of every Japanese child's education. And probably because of this wide dissemination, which continues in Japanese schools to the present day, many of the views presented in *Tsurezuregusa* have become part of the cultural outlook of the average Japanese.

The foreigner living in Japan who reads *Tsurezuregusa*, whether in the original or in Donald Keene's excellent translation, cannot help being struck by the similarity between certain attitudes of his Japanese friends and neighbors today and those of the fourteenth-century Buddhist priest Yoshida Kenkô. The emphasis on reserve in human relationships, the disdain for people who push themselves forward and make themselves conspicuous in a group—these are qualities which are familiar to us from day-to-day contact with the Japanese. They are also qualities which Yoshida Kenkô emphasized in *Tsurezuregusa*. The stress on the incomplete, the imperfect, the irregular as an esthetic ideal, noticeable in many art forms for centuries in Japan, is advocated in Kenkô's book, too. Praise for the beauty of simple things, traditionally an important element in Japanese esthetics, is found here as well. It would be hard to find a work which better reflects the esthetic ideals of the middle ages in Japan. Perhaps too it would be hard to find a book which has done more to make these ideals a part of the everyday lives of the Japanese.

Yoshida Kenkô looked back on the "good old days" of the aristocratic Heian culture with a nostalgia perhaps surprising in a Buddhist monk who had renounced the world. His detailed accounts of places, objects and events which reflected the glory of the old capital are probably the sections least interesting to modern readers, but even here one is impressed by his appreciative awareness of things. Whether describing the moonlight shining through the tops of cedar trees, or the interior of a tasteful Japanese house, or an old court ceremony, Kenkô shows a consciousness and sensitivity found only in the best writers. With this same power of perception, he moves easily from esthetic considerations to the world of human behavior, displaying an acute sense of what is tasteful in human relationships.

Westerners reading this book can discover how deeply rooted are some present-day Japanese ideals in esthetics and human conduct. Japanese rereading this book can come into contact once again with one of the formative influences on their cultural values. Anyone reading this book can delight in the sensitive reflections of one human being on the people and things around him, expressed in a fluid, lyrical style.

[Note] YOSHIDA KENKÔ (ca.1283~ca.1353) was .born into a family of *Shintô* priests, and acquired the culture and education proper to the aristocracy. At the age of thirty, after serving at court for a while, he became a Buddhist monk and began to live a life of seclusion.

Tsurezuregusa (*Essays in Idleness*) expresses his views on life, love, nature, his state of mind while living in retirement, and so forth, written down according to a free association of ideas. This style of writing belongs to the Japanese literary genre known as *zuihitsu*, and is popular with many Japanese even today. His Buddhist view that "everything is passing" is something else that contemporary Japanese feel quite familiar with.

Soga Monogatari—

Heroes and Villains

THOMAS J. COGAN

On a rainy night in the spring of 1193, the two Soga brothers, Jûrô, age 22, and Gorô, age 20, secretly entered the hunting camp of Minamoto no Yoritomo at the foot of Mount Fuji. Once inside, they proceeded to attack the quarters of their enemy, Suketsune, who had plotted the assassination of their father eighteen years before. After successfully completing the revenge, the elder brother was killed by a guard, and the younger one was captured, only to be beheaded later by the son of Suketsune.

Even though this incident occurred more than 800 years ago, the legacy of the two brothers is still alive. Every year on the 28th of May at a shrine near Odawara City southwest of Tokyo, various interested people, including a descendant of the family, perform rites and say prayers in memory of the brothers. In addition, there is even a Society for the Preservation of the Soga Brothers' Historic Places. Most Japanese know the outline of the Soga story; and during the 800 year interval it has provided material for numerous stories, poems, and plays. In both the literature dealing with the Soga revenge and the popular image, Jûrô and Gorô are seen as the heroes, while their foe, Suketsune, is obviously judged the villain. But is this a fair evaluation of the people involved in the story? I think not.

The origin of the Soga-Suketsune dispute centered around a land feud dating back several generations. In short, the Soga brothers' grandfather illegally seized both the land and the wife of Suketsune. Enraged by such blatant acts, Suketsune plotted revenge: the deaths of the grandfather and the father. Even though he entrusted the revenge to two of his loyal retainers, the assassins succeeded only in killing the boys' father. This act was the beginning of the desire for revenge that consumed the lives of the two brothers. However, according to the code of the warrior, Suketsune also had sufficient grounds for revenge, and yet, seldom does he receive anything but the villain's role in the legend.

It seems that Japanese heroes are not usually judged on the criteria of right or wrong, but rather on more personal and emotional grounds. In order to qualify as a hero, one has to have several attributes: dedication to a cause, sincerity, and purity of motive; in other words, selflessness. Such characteristics are more significant in the public mind than the legal issues of guilt and innocence. For the most part, the above generalization has held true from ancient times down to the present day.

This is one aspect of the Japanese psychology that strikes some Westerners as unique. Needless to say, in the West the choice between emotion and reason often arises; however, I think that the emotional side dominates in the evaluation of heroes more often in Japan. A person can legally be a villain but actually a hero, if such qualities as devotion, sincerity, and selflessness are discernible in his character. Thus, in spite of a rather dubious legal case, the Soga brothers have, down through the ages, been considered by most Japanese as heroes. It is my opinion that a closer look at the facts of the story would perhaps lessen to a certain extent the "villain" image of Suketsune. The two brothers will probably remain the heroes, but the distance separating the popular conception of them and the popular conception of Suketsune might decrease.

[Note] *Soga Monogatari* (*The Tale of the Soga Brothers*) is a heroic story dating back to the middle ages, telling of the revenge accomplished by the Soga brothers on their father's enemy at the foot of Mount Fuji, after suffering more than eighteen years of hardships. The author is unknown, but the story is presumed to have been composed by a Buddhist priest and then passed down to succeeding generations. The *Soga Monogatari* was recited by blind women entertainers, and became widely diffused among the common people. The story provided subject matter for *noh* recitations and the dances of the medieval period, as well as for the ballad dramas (*jōruri*) and *kabuki* plays of later centuries. The tragic story of powerless people who suffer with resignation, then accomplish their goal and are killed for doing so, has always appealed strongly to the feelings of the Japanese.

ZE'AMI —

An Ageless Theatrical Superstar

DON KENNY

My father is a minister of one of the Protestant sects. I was raised working alongside him producing the weekly church services for the congregations of various small towns throughout the Old West— Nebraska, Kansas, Oklahoma, and Wyoming. From the time I was eight or nine years old, I played the piano and organ, directed the choir, sang solos, directed weddings and funerals, and even preached occasionally for Dad when he was ill or suddenly called out of town.

Very early in my career, I began to think of this work as the production of weekly shows, and to study and experiment to discover the best means by which an audience can be moved and how to hold their interest and attention. I found that the most important key to success on the stage is hard training and perfection in rehearsal, and a cool head and total concentration during performance. And that the performer must use and control his emotional feelings while working, for the minute he lets these feelings take over and carry him away into ecstacy, his audience is left behind wondering what happened. They may be *impressed* by an emotional rendition, but they are only *moved* by a controlled one.

I went on to perform in school plays and musicals throughout my lower school days, and went to the university to train to become an opera singer. After graduating from the university, I was sent to Japan as a junior officer in the United States Navy.

It was here in Japan that I found theater that trains actors from the outside in. I became fascinated by *kabuki* and studied Japanese dance for six years. But I gradually found myself drawn to *kyôgen,* and have now studied it exclusively for close to ten years with Nomura Mansaku, who was recently designated a Living National Treasure. *Kyôgen* brought me more and more into contact with *noh* and Ze'ami.

To me, the ideal "theatrician" (total man of the theater) is one who has trained himself and experienced all four of the basic practical aspects of the craft of theater—actor, playwright, director and critic. The ideal actor has complete vocal, physical and spatial flexibility and control. The ideal playwright can structure and pattern time and has a deep understanding of language and human nature. The ideal director has the ability to create spatial composition and rhythm. And the ideal critic has a vast store of knowledge of the history and texture of all the arts, a highly refined sense of appropriateness, and an unemotionally analytical intellect.

It is well known that such men as the Greek tragedians, the classical masters Molière and Shakespeare, and modern film makers like Buster Keaton and Orson Welles all wrote, directed, and starred (or at least acted) in their own works. However, none of these men have left us any important theoretical or critical treatises concerning their art from an unemotionally detached viewpoint.

Ze'ami Motokiyo (1362?-1443) is the only man I have been able to find whose work and the records of whose life and activities seem to indicate that he qualifies as my ideal theatrician.

The honors that were heaped upon him by the Ashikaga Shogunate, and the manner in which he was lauded and/or criticized in the diaries and documents of the intelligentsia and literati of his day indicate that he was a great actor.

The numerous scripts (no agreement has been reached on the exact number he actually wrote) still performed today show that he was a poet-playwright of profound genius. His choreography, music, and economy of expression that have been physically passed down through the generations in the bodies of *noh* actors show that he was an expert director. And his sixteen theses present astute commentary on all aspects of practical theater—writing, directing, actor training, audience handling, and program planning—as well as incisive criticism of the work of the actors of the day, including his own family and himself. He also goes into the thought behind the practical aspect of life in the theater and the significance of that work in terms of religion and philosophy.

Ze'ami's work teems with theatrical truth and artistic vitality. He far exceeds my demands for the ideal theatrician, and is something of a universal, ageless theatrical superstar.

[Note] *Noh* is one of Japan's unique theatrical forms, taking its origin from two sources. It developed in part from mimicry and acrobatic performances imported from China during the T'ang dynasty, and in part from dances performed in farming communities to implore the gods for a good harvest. The man who combined the best features of these two sources and came up with the original form of the *noh* drama as it is performed today was Kan'ami, and his son Ze'ami brought the form to completion.

ZE'AMI (1362?-1443), besides being the outstanding playwright of *noh* dramas, was an accomplished actor and director, and has left some extraordinary prose in his literary criticism developing the theory of *noh*. The esthetic ideal expressed there is frequently referred to as *yûgen*, a kind of mysterious beauty.

Tauye Zôshi—

Poetry as Magic

Many Japanese may wonder why a foreigner would be interested enough in what may appear to be an insignificant aspect of Japanese culture to spend four to five years studying and translating the *Tauye Zôshi* (*A Collection of Rice-Planters' Songs*). I say 'insignificant' because I am particularly aware of the tendency for students of Japanese culture outside Japan, and consequently, the general reading public there as well, to measure items in Japanese culture along a scale determined by a pseudo-classical canon of "great works." Needless to say, I greatly regret the tendency though I am aware of its inevitability.

Although I want to speak of magic and poetry, a topic of general interest in Western poetics at least from the time of the French poet Rimbaud, I think that I can most easily lay the groundwork for this by comparing a song in the *Tauye Zôshi* to that accompanying agricultural labor in another culture, the Trobriand Islands, as recorded by the important anthropologist Malinowski.

This song is from the first set of noon songs in the *Tauye Zôshi*.
Flowers on the chestnut tree bloomed thick . . . .
Flowers on the chestnut tree in bloom made bright a whole hillside.

At first glance this verse appears to be merely descriptive of a spring landscape, but the following from an instruction book recorded at Mibu, Chiyoda-machi, Hiroshima Prefecture draws our attention to what might be called the "symbolic" meaning of the verse.

First set of noon songs: Write about flowers blooming on trees and shrubs. The brightness of the sun, flowers blooming, a young man when he is seventeen or eighteen. All these beautiful things. Have these in mind when you sing. The month is the fifth month.

This quotation mentions a quality of the poetry of the *Tauye Zôshi* for which the expression "magical function" seems to me more appropriate than "symbolic meaning." Malinowski makes clear the magical function of poetry in work songs in the following comment on what farmers in the Trobriand Islands sing as they work over their own vegetable gardens. The spell he refers to is:

Millipede here now, millipede here ever . . . The millipede shoots along, shoots along . . . Shoot up, O head of my *tayutu* . . .

"This clear and beautiful spell takes the millipede as its leading word because of its rapidity of movement. The millipede is also associated with the magical and mythological cycle of ideas concerning rain and cloud, since it is a prognostic of downpour. Hence the millipede is also a symbol of fertility. In the middle part the direct aim of this magic—the development of the *tayutu* plant above ground and in the soil—is clearly expressed. In the last part the stress is placed on the branches."

Set side by side in this way, the two passages—Malinowski commenting on the magic of song performed in an agricultural work setting in the Trobriand Islands, and instructions to Japanese farmers on what to sing about at the time of rice planting—remind us of something we had forgotten about poetry: it really does work. Poetry produces things. At least, the people in these two different cultures—one rice, the other various types of potatoes and yams—arranged that their field work and song should coincide in such a way that once each year, at the proper season, speech or song—their very breath—was one with the purpose of their body's efforts, the production of food on which to live. In this way they claimed a place for themselves in the cycle of nature. I suppose that the reason I have been interested in the *Tauye Zôshi* has been my own effort to be close, if only imaginatively and not actually—since I do live in a city and in an industrialized age—to an arrangement such as this one. I participate in their myth by studying and translating their songs.

[Note] *Tauye Zôshi* is a collections of traditional songs sung in Japanese farming villages during the rice-planting season. It is estimated that they were put together during the sixteenth and seventeenth centuries.

Rice is the source of life for Japanese, and so the planting of young rice-plants was the most important event of the year in farming villages. Besides being strenuous labor which required the cooperation of the entire village, it was also a religious festival to pray for a good harvest. The rice-planting songs are both work songs and religious festival songs.

IHARA SAIKAKU —

The Spirit of the Japanese Renaissance

NATALIA JVANENKO

It is impossible to speak of all the works of the great writer Ihara Saikaku in so short an essay. I shall discuss only his unexcelled *Shokokubanashi* (*Tales from the Several Provinces*). I have been interested in this collection of short stories for a very long time. The Japanese renaissance spirit is particularly well expressed in it. This is not my opinion alone. Many Japanese and foreign scholars have made comparative analyses of the beautiful girl whose lover is murdered, and have seen in Boccaccio's Ghismonda, and Saikaku's "*Song of the Fan of Love*" (*Shinobi Ôgi no Chôka*) a similarity between the Japanese and Renaissance conceptions. But I would like to add a few words to the discussion.

In both the *Decameron* and Saikaku's *Tales from the Several Provinces* the genre is the novella, which, in its proper meaning of short story, arose in Renaissance Italy. It was in the beginning a literary form which, while it valued realistic detail still favored an interesting story over a realistic one. Plot itself originated in legend and fable, in which there was no clear boundary between fiction and reality. We must not, however, forget that in Boccaccio's time and Saikaku's too a kind of imagining was taken as reality. For example, the dreams that foretell events and the illusory appearances of reality in Boccaccio can not have been real, but almost everyone believed in them and in the power of magic as well. The lizard which in the Saikaku legend turns itself into a monstrous creature to have its revenge upon the noble lady into whose wall it has been nailed was to the reader of the day real.

We have on the other hand works like the unique short story "*The Golden Pot Left Over*" (*Nokorumono tote Kin no Nabe*) in which Saikaku invented monsters and aimed at exaggeration and the unusual itself. He could go on to skillful parody as in *"When the Thunder God was Ill"* (*Kaminari no Byôchû*).

The theme that runs through the collection is, as Saikaku himself wrote in the introduction, "The world in all its breadth." The mood of each of the stories comes from Saikaku's emotional response to the breadth and variety of the world. Thus in *"The Lotus Leaf Five Yards Across"* (*Hachijôjiki no Hasu no Ha*), a priest called Sakugen tells Oda Nobunaga of seeing a lotus leaf in India big enough for a man to sleep on. Nobunaga does not believe the story and has him ejected, whereupon he bursts into tears. When Nobunaga's retainers ask if he is weeping tears of chagrin, he answers, "Not at all. Tears of sorrow, rather, that the great man who rules over the land should be of such narrow vision." The exaggeration seems to me beautifully expressive of the world that was Saikaku's inspiration.

Another theme of the collection is, again in Saikaku's words, that "people are apparitions." I would rephrase it: "People are the strangest creatures in the world." Saikaku's enormous fascination with the reason, knowledge, and power of the human being dominates many of the stories. A blind man who can unerringly identify approaching footsteps, a young man who by dint of strict training is strong enough to lift a cow, a monk who manages in complete silence to steal a drum from a temple, a samurai who runs his opponent through even though he himself has fallen—these are among the characters who people Saikaku's world.

Another point of interest is that in this collection the fragmentary and elliptical expressions that derive from satirical linked verse and fill *The Life of an Amorous Woman* (*Kôshoku Ichidai Onna*) and *The Eternal Storehouse of Japan* (*Nippon Eitaigura*) and others of Saikaku's works are almost completely absent. The style is extremely simple, the contemporary colloquial is used, puns and associative words and specifically literary parody and allusion are completely absent. But the spirit of satirical linked verse is, it seems to me, a matter more of content than of style, and parody is of the essence; and of that there is rather a good deal in this collection too. *"Test of Strength in the Clouds"* (*Unchû no Udeoshi*) is a perfect example.

The famous hero Yoshitsune is thoroughly bested by the beautiful Shizuka Gozen, his mistress.

I think this collection a masterpiece of the highest order even in comparison with other superior works by Saikaku.

(Tr. by Janine Beichman)

[Note] IHARA SAIKAKU (1642-1693) is recognized as the greatest fiction writer of the Edo period. He was born into a merchant family, and began his writing career as a prolific poet of *haiku*. After reaching the age of forty he turned to fiction, and in the ten years until his death wrote many outstanding works. His fiction can be divided into three general categories: books of love and sex, dealing with human passions; books that took *samurai* (with their special code of ethics) for their subject matter; and books about townspeople, treating the merchants and artisans of the towns and cities. Besides these there are collections of legends based on local traditions, such as *Tales from the Several Provinces*. In the preface to this book Saikaku wrote: "There are many strange phenomena in this world, but nothing quite so strange as man himself." This sums up Saikaku's extraordinary curiosity about people and his eagerness to study them deeply. Saikaku is highly esteemed even today as an outstanding writer of fiction because of his sharp observation of the society he lived in, and his vivid depiction of the realities of human life.

Matsuo Bashô—

The Rejection and Influence of Chinese Culture

Chen Shun-chen

"Many of the men of old died on the road . . ."

This sentence is contained in the opening paragraph of *The Narrow Inland Roads*. The commentators usually interpret these "men of old" to mean famous men of former times whom Bashô respected: Saigyô, Sôgi, Li Po, Tu Fu and others. Li Po spent ten of his middle years wandering in exile from the capital, Ch'ang-an. In his later years his death sentence was commuted and he was exiled to Kweichow. While on the way there he received an official pardon, and was journeying back when he died. Tu Fu set out for Szechwan in search of food during a famine, always dreaming of returning to the eastern capital, and he finally died on his way back, never reaching Ch'ang-an.

> I too. . . have been stirred by the sight of a solitary cloud
> drifting with the wind to ceaseless thoughts of roaming.

Bashô's notion of "travel" expressed here seems to be somewhat different from that of Li Po; and Tu Fu in particular did not set out on a journey by choice. Admittedly Li Po seems to have had "thoughts of roaming;" he wrote in a letter to the governor of Anchou that men should be ready to travel anywhere. But aesthetic considerations were secondary for him; a man's "determination" was the important motive for travel, and travel was simply a preparatory activity for the sake of useful participation in government. Tu Fu also earnestly sought office in the bureaucracy, and when he attained high office he always had the good of the nation in mind.

This consciousness of the nation seems never to have been very strong in Bashô, even though he himself claimed that he was following the spirit of Li Po and Tu Fu.

When he visited Nikkô, Bashô wrote:

As all begins afresh,
On the green leaves, on the young leaves
The brightness of the sun.[1]

But then he escaped, saying "feeling hesitant at such a place, I put aside my brush."

Bashô described *haiku* poems as being like "summer fires and winter fans." Summer fires and winter fans are completely useless things, removed from reality. Bashô held, then, that the further removed from reality a poem is, the deeper the spirit of *haiku*. Bashô, while strongly influenced by Li Po and Tu Fu, overlooked an important part of their poetics, namely their close adherence to the tradition that poetry expressed a person's will or determination (usually with political connotations). More correctly, Bashô probably ignored this aspect of their poetry on purpose. Precisely because he did not turn his attention in this direction, the roots of *haiku* were not influenced by Chinese literature, and one may say that the *haiku* developed as something distinctively Japanese.

And yet, in the very beginning of *The Narrow Inland Roads*, Li Po's "The months and days are the travelers of eternity" is quoted, and the poetry of Chinese poets is quoted throughout the work, for example Tu Fu's "Countries may fall, but their rivers and mountains remain." Also in the case of scenery, Bashô used as material famous Chinese places which he had never seen, such as Lake Tung-ting, Lake Si Hu, or the river Chekiang.

Japanese culture, while adopting elements of the more advanced Chinese culture, was not overwhelmed by it. Japan used Chinese culture as a point of reference, developing its own culture and advancing in its own direction. *The Narrow Inland Roads* may be taken as one of the most typical examples of this tendency. This work represents the most easily understandable pattern in a comparative study of the cultures of China and Japan. As such, it is a work I would recommend to any Chinese interested in studying Japan.

Among the poems in *The Narrow Inland Roads*, we find:

Whiter far than the white rocks
Of the Rock Temple

The autumn wind blows.[2]

This brings to mind the opening lines of Li Chang-chi's *Journey through Southern Mountains and Fields*: "The autumn fields are bright, the autumn wind white . . ." But on closer consideration, this similarity is in the manner of expression only. In Bashô's *haiku*, I can find little in common with the poetic sentiment expressed by Li Chang-chi. There are probably few examples of poems which present as clearly as these two such a similarity of expression combined with poetic views that are so completely different.

> The wild dark ocean:
> Streaming over it to Sado Island,
> The river of stars.[3]

In my opinion, this seems the most "Chinese" of all the *haiku* in *The Narrow Inland Roads*. In any case, even though Japan has taken many things from China, I feel that we may take as a starting point for the study of Japan the fact that Japan has never really used these elements of Chinese culture in making a composite picture of Japanese culture. For the study of Japanese culture, *The Narrow Inland Roads* provides material which deserves to be examined closely and repeatedly.   (Tr. by William Currie)

[Note] MATSUO BASHÔ (1644-1694) is Japan's outstanding *haiku* poet. Since his *haiku* invariably appear in the textbooks used for compulsory education in Japan, there are hardly any Japanese who are not familiar with the *haiku* of Bashô. He wrote five travel diaries, and of these, *The Narrow Inland Roads,* written towards the end of his life, is considered to be his masterpiece. He lived for travel, and died on a journey; life itself for him was a journey. The diaries he wrote and the poetry he composed were inspired by nature and the seasons, as well as by traces of history closely bound up with nature.

The *haiku* is a form of poetry very popular with many Japanese even today, and a form which has had considerable influence on contemporary poetry throughout the world.

(1)(3)Tr. by Earl Miner. The founder of the Tokugawa Shogunate is enshrined at Nikko. (2)Tr. by Yuasa Nobuyuki

CHIKAMATSU MONZAYEMON —

Japan's First Professional Dramatist

DONALD KEENE

Chikamatsu Monzayemon (1653-1724) is often ranked as the greatest Japanese playwright. His only rival for this distinction is Ze'ami, whose *noh* plays, though indisputable masterpieces, do not easily fit any usual definition of drama. Chikamatsu, by contrast, was unmistakably a dramatist: he wrote his best works for the puppet theatre, but they were adopted for the *kabuki* stage, and in more recent times have been made into successful films. Although he faithfully described a society that has all but vanished, the griefs of his characters have universal validity, and a performance of one of his masterpieces continues to be a moving experience, even without the modernization to which they have so often been subjected.

Chikamatsu is credited by some scholars with as many as 160 plays, but even if this figure is inflated, he undoubtedly wrote an exceptionally large number. Before Chikamatsu both the *kabuki* and puppet theatres performed plays which, as surviving texts indicate, were undistinguished, if not childish. Each theatre exploited its special forte: *kabuki* tended to be a display of virtuoso acting techniques, but the puppet plays, taking advantage of the expendability of the puppets, often included scenes of mayhem or prodigies of strength. The atmosphere of *kabuki* was generally cheerful, even when the plots involved tragic actions, but the puppet theatre relied on gloomier, more distinctly Buddhist themes. It was not attempted to create works of permanent value for either theatre, and the playbooks, as if reflecting the insignificance of the authors, were left unsigned.

This situation was entirely changed by Chikamatsu. Although he was a *samurai* by birth and at one time served in the household of a Kyoto nobleman, he was not ashamed to affix his name to his works.

Probably his first play was *Yotsugi Soga* (*The Soga Heir*) written in 1683 for the puppet theatre. The instant success of the work established Chikamatsu's fame. For the first time a dramatist, rather than an actor or a chanter of the puppet theatre, was the central factor in the success of a play. *Yotsugi Soga* is by no means a memorable work, but it contains unconventional scenes that display Chikamatsu's burgeoning mastery of the medium, and some passages are written in a language that lifted the puppet play for the first time to the level of literature. His next important puppet play, *Shusse Kagekiyo* (*Kagekiyo Victorious*, 1686), was even more experimental. The tone of the play, for all the heroic deeds, is almost uniformly dark, and the character Akoya is a part worthy of a great performer. Although the play as a whole does not bear comparison with the masterpieces of Chikamatsu's mature period, it has a tragic intensity that he would not again achieve. Akoya is a believable woman with the contradictions and complexities that distinguish a human being from a puppet, a character of such depth as to break the permissible limits of a puppet play. That may be why *Shusse Kagekiyo*, though today recognized as the first work of the "new" puppet drama, attracted comparatively little attention in its day.

Chikamatsu continued to the end of his career to write historical plays about the celebrated figures of the Japanese past, but he is admired chiefly for his domestic dramas about the ordinary Osaka townsmen of his day. *Sonezaki Shinjû* (*The Love Suicides at Sonezaki*, 1703), written within a fortnight of the suicides Chikamatsu described, elevated the deaths of a shop assistant and a prostitute to the level of tragedy by the skill of the construction and the splendid poetry of the descriptive passages. His most popular work, *Kokusen'ya Kassen* (*The Battles of Coxinga*, 1715) was a melodrama loosely based on the career of the Chinese-Japanese adventurer Cheng Ch'eng-kung who attempted to restore the Ming Dynasty in China. It is filled with bombast and exaggerated gestures, but it is so ingeniously written that it maintains its popularity to this day. Chikamatsu's single masterpiece was *Shinjû Ten no Amijima* (*The Love Suicides at Amijima*, 1720), a deeply affecting domestic tragedy.

Chikamatsu's views on the art of the puppet theatre were preserved in *Naniwa Miyage*, a work published by a friend in 1738. This account of a conversation with Chikamatsu contains the famous remark that "art lies within the slender margin between the real and the unreal," a statement that helps to explain why Chikamatsu's works written for the puppet theatre with its special demands were able to transcend such limitations and achieve the stature of true drama.

[Note] CHIKAMATSU MONZAYEMON (1653-1724) came from a *samurai* background, and became a playwright for the puppet theater in Kyoto when he was close to thirty. During the next forty years of his life, until his death at the age of seventy-two, he wrote more than one hundred puppet plays and over thirty *kabuki* dramas. Together with the master story-teller Ihara Saikaku and the great *haiku* poet Matsuo Bashô who were his contemporaries, Chikamatsu completes the trio of giants who established a golden age of literature in the Edo period.

Yosa Buson —

Great Teacher and Reformer of *Haiku*

Leon M. Zolbrod

The *haiku* movement aimed at making the art of poetry accessible to everyone, and Bashô and Buson were its outstanding masters. A goodly amount of material is now available to the English-speaking reader who wants to learn about the seventeenth-century poet, but comparatively little may be found on his eighteenth-century follower, who in many ways worked to preserve the memory and traditions of the Bashô school.

Indeed, if Bashô may be thought of as Moses, the giver of the law, Buson brings to mind Jesus, the great teacher and reformer. Moreover, not only did Buson succeed in renovating the world of *haiku* poetry nearly a century after Bashô's death, but he also made his mark as an outstanding painter who helped to introduce the Chinese manner known as the "literary style." No one in all of Japanese history more superbly combined excellence in these two arts.

Above all, Buson was a reluctant genius, hesitant to push himself to the leadership of his group of followers. He preferred to avoid public fame and honor, accepting his responsibilities only when they were irrevocably thrust on him at the beginning of the 1770's. But once he became the head of "The Midnight Hut" (*Yahantei*, as his group was called), he worked tirelessly to bring this new form of poetry closer to the old one of *waka*, thus fulfilling one of Bashô's unrealized ideals that poetry should be for everyone.

Already in his earliest verses, such as,

> Willow leaves are gone,
> The clear waters have dried up—
> Rocks scattered here and there,
> (*Yanagi chiri/ shimizu kare, ishi/tokoro dokoro.*)

composed during his decade of wandering, like Bashô, in the north-

eastern part of Japan, one finds a suggestion of his later mature style.
He brings together an impeccable ear for the rhythms of language, a
concise imagistic focus on the meaningful features of the world of
nature, and a realization of the nostalgic attraction of the early
medieval poet-monk, Saigyô, who wrote in similar terms at the same
spot about pausing by the banks of a clear brook and resting under
the shade of a willow tree.

Buson immortalized the world of his childhood, amid the rural
delta area of the Yodo River, near Osaka, where the land and the sea
meet, in these two famous verses:

> The sea in the spring—
> All day long it rises and falls,
> Just rises and falls.
>
> (*Haru no umi/ hinemosu notari/ notari kana.*)

And

> Fields of rape in bloom—
> The moon in the eastern sky;
> Sunset in the west.
>
> (*Na no hana ya/ tsuki wa higashi ni/ hi wa nishi ni.*)

The first of these captures the promise of the fertile sea that with
each new year a fresh cycle of life will begin in a gently undulating
movement suggesting the archetypal power of creation. In the second,
the heavenly bodies of the sun and moon, the products of mother
earth, and the works of man—who plants the bright yellow fields for
his food and fuel—are combined with a sense of the passage of time.
No wonder Buson has been called the poet of spring and praised for
his romantic spirit.

Yet the realization that all which flowers must fade, integral to the
Buddhist viewpoint, did not escape Buson's consciousness, as the
following verse indicates:

> Fallen peonies
> Piled one on top another—
> Two or three petals.
>
> (*Botan chitte/ uchi-kasanari nu/ ni-san pen.*)

In these royal Chinese blossoms one finds an exotic touch, at once delicate or even decadent in its beauty, hinting paradoxically that enduring strength comes from combining the best of disparate civilizations. As the blossom drops from the stem, one actually feels a sense of relief and recognizes that this event is necessary if life is to go on.

In contrast with Bashô, no single verse by Buson can represent all that the poet stood for, but the last three haiku above most nearly exemplify the qualities that make him deserving of the close attention of all students of Japanese literature.

[Note] YOSA BUSON (1716-1783), together with Bashô, is one of the great masters of *haiku* poetry. Born about one hundred years after Bashô, he gave fresh new life to the *haiku* style which Bashô had perfected, but which had fallen into decline. Characteristic of Buson's style is his skill in expressing images which are like paintings, and the colorful estheticism which appears frequently in his *haiku*.

Uyeda Akinari—

The Art of the Ghost Story

Anthony H. Chambers

The tales in Uyeda Akinari's *Ugetsu Monogatari* are the best representatives of the multitude of Japanese ghost stories. But they are not ordinary ghost stories. The collection is provocative, subtle and chilling, a beautifully crafted work of art and one of the most intriguing works of Japanese literature.

In a sense the *Ugetsu* tales are not ghost stories at all, because Akinari's main interest was in the dreams, the fears, the passions and disappointments of his characters. We see the sad disillusionment of a loyal subject who meets the depraved ghost of his former emperor; the fulfillment of an artist-priest who takes on the shape of the fish he loves to paint; and the ferocious wrath of a wife abandoned by her dissipated husband. The psychological truth in Akinari's portrayals and the author's compassion for his characters help to raise this collection far above the level of the ordinary ghost story.

Akinari covers the whole spectrum of traditional Japanese society, from the vengeful ghost of Emperor Sutoku to priests, *samurai*, merchants and peasants. *Ugetsu* is fascinating in its variety. With gentle irony Akinari explores relationships between ruler and subject, husband and wife, friend and friend, father and son, man and nature, even man and money—and of course between man and the supernatural.

The supernatural has many aspects: metamorphosis, wrathful ghosts, gentle loving ghosts, the spirit of wealth, and the spirit of a lecherous snake. In *Aozukin* (*The Blue Hood*) the power of Zen Buddhism cures a mad priest of his necrophilia. While the tale has the trappings of the supernatural, it can be read as a sensitive study in abnormal psychology.

The *Ugetsu* tales are suffused with great poetic beauty—the sinister, suggestive beauty conveyed by the title, which means "Tales of a Clouded Moon" or "Tales of Moonlight and Rain." And they are alive with a sense of wonder at the beauty and horror of all that is beyond man's understanding and control.

Throughout the collection Akinari maintains a delicate balance between fantasy and history. All of the stories hover on the margin of dream and reality, and remind us that distinctions between illusion and truth are not as clear as we would like to think. More fanciful ghost stories, less faithful to history and less sensitive to the subtleties of human psychology, would not stimulate the reader's imagination as Akinari's tales do.

Many of the stories demonstrate the power that passion and lust have over men. The spiteful ghost of Emperor Sutoku ferments civil war to get revenge on his enemies, and the great priest Saigyô is unable to dissuade him. A greedy peasant leaves his devoted wife in a vain pursuit of wealth. The priest-turned-fish succumbs to the pangs of hunger and swallows the fisherman's bait. A handsome young scholar is bewitched by a lascivious snake. And a virtuous priest devours the corpse of his young lover.

In every story the power of virtue is brought to bear against man's foolishness and greed, but Akinari knew that virtue does not always win out over human passions. It is this awareness that makes *Ugetsu Monogatari* a profoundly moving, troubling and human work.

[Note] UYEDA AKINARI (1734-1809) was a literary scholar and a poet as well as a writer of fiction. His masterpiece is *Ugetsu Monogatari* (*Tales of Moonlight and Rain*), made up of nine short tales of the supernatural. Taking material from Chinese and Japanese classical literature, he created these tales of mystery with originally conceived plots. The stories present a world of dreams described with an elegant, concise prose style, and they represent one of the finest achievements of Edo literature. These tales have also had an influence on modern Japanese fiction, as may be seen in the writings of Izumi Kyôka, Satô Haruo, Mishima Yukio and others.

HIGUCHI ICHIYÔ—

Nameless and Faceless Women

MARGARET YAMASHITA

Higuchi Ichiyô was born in 1872 and died twenty-four years later, in 1896. She was a writer and a woman in a time when neither had quite reached the level of respectability; it is doubtful in Japan that the latter has even today.

Ichiyô—her pen name—wrote a comparatively small volume of prose (she earlier wrote some undistinguished poetry), of which little is of enduring quality. But that small quantity ranks with Japan's best. The subject matter of Ichiyô's prose deals primarily with the downtrodden of her sex—the bar-girls, the budding prostitutes, the unhappily married. Not until the very end of her life were her accomplishments recognized, but when they were, and by that most distinguished writer and critic Mori Ôgai, her place in Japanese literature was secured.

Higuchi Ichiyô was called the "last woman of old Japan" by Sôma Gyofû and a "real poet" by Mori Ôgai. To this we should add that she also was a social critic and, perhaps Japan's first advocate of women's liberation. These qualities may seem the very antithesis of each other. They are, and yet Ichiyô was able to combine them skilfully in some very successful novels. I should like, therefore, to discuss them briefly as they figure in *Jûsan'ya* (*The Thirteenth Night*).

O-seki, a woman from a poor and humble family, is unhappily married to a rich but unkind man, Harada. On the thirteenth night of September (by the lunar calendar), a traditional harvest moon-viewing evening, O-seki decides to leave Harada and their son Tarô and return to her parents' house. She visits them on this evening and tells them of her resolution, but they persuade her to put aside her pride and return to her husband for the sake of her own family, whom Harada has benefited. On her way back O-seki discovers that her *jinrikisha*[1] puller is a childhood friend of hers, a man whom she had once wished to marry. Since then he too has made an unsuccessful marriage and has sunk to the depths of poverty. They meet for a moment, bound by their common grief, and then part.

The plot, as we can see, is very simple; *Jûsan'ya* is rather more an examination of the characters' emotions and reactions. In this respect, O-seki, the main character, is disappointing to the liberated reader. Why? Because she has no resolve, no determination; she is easily dissuaded from her decision to leave Harada. O-seki is a faceless, nameless person; we feel pity but we do not know for whom. But of course, this is exactly the point that Ichiyô is trying to convey: the facelessness and namelessness of Japanese women made so by Japanese society. O-seki's fate is a perfect example of the unjust treatment of women by her society. But then, you ask, what about her childhood friend? He too is a victim of society. Yes. Even men are not immune from the mistreatment of society. But the choice to leave his wife was his—he does have slightly more freedom. What about O-seki's father? It was he who persuaded her to go back to Harada, yet he cannot be faulted for deliberate cruelty, only for being an unwitting pawn of the society which has taught him to suppress compassion for his own daughter. Only Harada appears to be intentionally unkind. Or perhaps he is a caricature of the typical Japanese husband, cruel in his thoughtlessness, in his inability to consider his wife as much a human being as himself. Both reasons are equally unflattering and equally condemning.

Ichiyô does not suggest solutions; she only delineates the problem. The problem of *Jûsan'ya* is the absence of rights for the married woman in Japanese society. Ichiyô here has captured the essence of this injustice and has focussed upon it with a poignancy not easily forgotten. Our hackles are raised, the more so in realizing the futility of opposing tradition. It is an enduring cruelty. Ichiyô articulated the plea for justice in her time; it was noticed but not acted upon.

[Note] HIGUCHI ICHIYÔ (1872-1896) is recognized as a woman writer of exceptional ability who appeared in the earliest period of modern Japanese literature. At the age of eighteen, when her father died and her family was reduced to poverty, she began operating a small shop. At the same time she was writing poetry and fiction, and won the high praise of Mori Ôgai for her novella *Takekurabe* (literally, "comparing heights"; translated into English as *Growing Up*). Ôgai's praise, however, did not help her out of her poverty. As a result of overwork she contracted a lung disease and died at the age of twenty-four. Because her career was so brief, she left only a few short pieces and diaries, but her reputation remains high even today. She is considered to be one of the bright lights in the history of Japanese literature.

Jûsan'ya (*The Thirteenth Night*) was written when she was twenty-three. It contains her protest against the subjection of women and also against the tyranny of the ruling class, both of which were prevalent at that time. She sets her tragedy skillfully and with artistic effect against a background of willows and pampas grass waving in the light of the harvest moon.

1. A man-pulled cart

Masaoka Shiki—

The First Modern *Haiku* Poet

Janine Beichman

Masaoka Shiki (1867-1902) is popularly ranked with Bashô, Buson and Issa as one of the four greatest *haiku* poets of Japan. When asked about his historical importance, most people would reply that it lies in the creation of *shasei*, a form of realism. Although this is not quite accurate, it is still true that Shiki was the first to apply to *haiku* the doctrines of realism that circulated in the art and literary worlds during the first half of the Meiji period. However, to assume that Shiki's accomplishment ended there ignores what seems to me the most revolutionary quality of his poetry: the creation of a modern persona as its speaker.

Shiki's *haiku* (some, not all) possess a combination of two qualities that can not be found in any *haiku* poet before him: the presumption of an almost physical intimacy between the poet and his audience, and, at the same time, a distance of the poet from himself that is based on a high degree of objective self-awareness. The following poem which, like all his best work, is autobiographical, illustrates my point:

Yomei	How much life
ikubaku ka aru	is left me now?
Yo mijikashi	Brief, these summer nights . . .

The first two lines are a question the poet poses (to whom is unclear), perhaps whispering the words or only thinking them in his mind. The last line is a "season word," and tells us that the poem takes place as the sun rises on a hot summer dawn. Yet if that were all there were to the poem, there would be nothing extraordinary about it. What makes it extraordinary is the evocative relation between the poet's question and the purely descriptive phrase which becomes its reply.

It helps to know that when Shiki wrote this poem he was an invalid, suffering from incurable tuberculosis and its complications. It was probably his pain, which never ceased for long, that had awakened him at dawn, reminding him that he had not much longer to live (he died at thirty-five). Perhaps his comment on the brevity of the summer night was meant to allude to the brevity of his own life. In any case, it seems an apt accompaniment to his question. Yet, there is more to the poem than this.

The poem is undoubtedly meant to evoke a sense of evanescence, and to make the reader see a sort of double exposure image wherein Shiki's own brief life is merged with the fleeting summer night. Still, one wonders, what was Shiki's reaction to this? The poem itself does not explicitly tell us if Shiki longed for death as a respite from his suffering, if he regretted its imminence, or if he simply accepted it. Did he wish to die, did he wish to live, or had he achieved a state in which he was beyond all desire? The poem, in the end, leaves room for all three emotions to coexist, as they did, in reality, in Shiki.

Because the time of the poem is dawn, when all is hushed and almost everyone is asleep, the reader can not help imagining that the poet is talking to himself or, at the most, to a close friend or nurse who had spent the night beside him. His voice seems soft, almost a whisper in the heart. He might even be addressing the Great Void while all humankind sleeps; but I prefer to think that he is posing the question of his own mortality in his mind and allowing the reader to overhear his thoughts. Shiki is speaking here not as an artist but as a sick man, and the tone is completely private. He assumes an extraordinary intimacy with his audience; rather than reporting on what passed through his mind in general terms and after the fact, he lets the poem's audience listen in as he is in the process of thinking. Yet, at the same time, he maintains an objective distance from himself, and it is this which gives the poem its restraint, a restraint that contrasts strangely with its intimate tone.

If there is a continuum from the private to the public along which one may progress by gradually adding more and more clothing to one's naked emotions, then Shiki sought to capture himself much earlier along on that continuum than had earlier poets. That is why he so often dispensed with metaphor, simile, and other tropes. He wished to depict himself emotionally naked; yet he did so with an objectivity and self-awareness that saves his work from vulgarity. In place of Bashô's beautiful imagery, Buson's striking verbal pictures, and Issa's poignant sentiments, Shiki offered a new psychological complexity and a wholly modern relation with the reader that no Japanese *haiku* poet had achieved before him.

[Note] MASAOKA SHIKI (1867-1902) came to Tokyo from the countryside hoping to become a politician, then became interested in literature and wrote some fiction, but was never recognized as a novelist. Turning to *haiku* and *tanka*, however, he brought about a major reform, giving these traditional forms of poetry a new life in the modern period both by his poems and his criticism. His influence is still felt on present-day *haiku* and *tanka*.

Shiki was a friend of Natsume Sôseki's, and was the first one to encourage him to write novels. Soon after the success of his first novel, Sôseki turned to writing as a professional career.

Mori Ôgai—

The Sordid and the Beautiful

Sanford Goldstein

It is perhaps strange to juxtapose Ôgai's *The Wild Geese* and *Vita Sexualis*, for at first glance the stories seem so utterly dissimilar. The former is about the plight of a girl sold into the position of a mistress in order to support her father in his old age; the latter concerns the evolution of the sexual life of its hero, but with a philosophical complexity built into the pattern. When the Westerner realizes the two stories are by the same author, he may perhaps feel, in the same way one does about reading Mishima's *The Sound of Waves* (1954) and *The Temple of the Golden Pavilion* (1956), that the simpler story was written earlier. But we have to cut across the convenient analytical pattern, for *Vita* was published in 1909, *Geese* in twelve issues of *Subaru* (*The Pleiades*) over a two-year period between 1911 and 1913.

A reviewer once said *The Wild Geese* was "one of the most unusual and thoroughly charming stories" he had read in years. It seems doubtful that anyone would make the same claim for *Vita*, yet its lack of explicit sexual detail offers a peculiar charm of its own. That the authorities banned its sale twenty-seven days after it appeared may surprise modern readers, *Vita* having none of the bold sexuality of such later writers as Mishima and Ôye, nor any of the frank depictions of sexual desire typical of Tayama Katai's *Bedding* (1907) and Iwano Hômei's *Debauchery* (1909). Ôgai himself expected the banning, his letter dated August 1, 1909, tersely asserting, "Ten years ago nude pictures were also treated in the same way, whether they deserved it or not. Ten years from now the authorities will wake up."

Books may be linked on any number of levels, but perhaps the linkage of *Geese* and *Vita* may be made through Ôgai's oft-stated criticism and rebellion against the Japanese naturalists who Ôgai felt were misrepresenting the actual ideas of Zola and Maupassant. If *Vita* is Ôgai's direct protest against the one-sided dimensionality of the naturalists, then *Geese* is his indirect protest even as he is here dealing with an aspect of the sordid that was perhaps commonplace in Meiji Japan and earlier. The innocent O-tama is first deceived by a policeman and then a usurer, and while her father has raised her with the greatest love and protection, the truth remains he does accept conditions which had to bring disgrace upon her. He is placed in a comfortable house of his own and given his own maid, and while he often waits like some Père Goriot for O-tama's visit, he sends her back with alacrity in order not to annoy *their* protector. It is the lovely heroine herself who goes out to entice the student Okada, ostensibly to thank him for having rescued one of her two birds from a snake that had attacked their cage. But like the hero of the earlier *Vita*, the student is about to leave for Germany, the mistress' plan of meeting him destroyed by the accident of the killing of a wild goose. The two young people never meet again, though the narrator, it seems, has been able to have some sort of intimate relationship with O-tama.

What Ôgai has managed to do as skilfully as the naturalists is to delineate the sexual in a number of incidents in both stories, especially in *Vita*, but he manages to focus on other elements in life to broaden the perspective, to keep the rational elements equally on the scene, to juxtapose the disagreeable with the pleasant, the sordid with the beautiful, the disharmonious with the tender. The moneylender's wife is seen holding a parasol that looks like a swaddling cloth carried at the end of a stick; at fourteen the hero-philosopher of *Vita* runs away from the suggestive advances of his friend's mother to a deserted spot where "clusters of trumpet flowers were blooming as if aflame" and where he pictures to himself "a multitude of images;" Okada passes the waiting O-tama, the lower part of his *kimono* "expanded in a curious way so that he looked like a circular cone" as he conceals the dead goose under his garment; at a marriage-interview *Vita*'s hero asks his hosts for buckwheat mash because of a painfully decaying tooth; and Suezô the moneylender partially calms his jealous wife by noting O-tama's face is too flat. In no instance does *Vita*'s hero allow sex to overwhelm him, his comments on the loss of his virginity typical of the controlled analysis through the book, and *Geese*'s young scholar apparently leaves for Germany with his own virtue intact, the reader's sympathy remaining with the image of the lonely O-tama standing on the slope by her house.

At the end of *Vita* the hero-narrator decides not to let his son read this sexual life the father has spent time recording; at the end of *Geese* the narrator refuses to disclose how he came in contact with O-tama. Both events suggest Ôgai's *via negativa*. This withholding of information, of the precise detail, of the sexually sordid—even as the author is being outspoken and precise and is depicting a world partially base—seems Ôgai-istic, Oriental, an aspect of the Japanese way, all of which may account for considering Ôgai one of Japan's most representative authors.

[Note] MORI ÔGAI (1862-1922) served as the Surgeon-General of the Japanese Army, and at the same time was an outstanding novelist, playwright, critic, and translator. Returning from studies in Germany, he did a great deal to introduce European literature and esthetics in Japan. At the same time he was writing his own novels, such as *The Girl Who Danced*. *Vita Sexualis* was written as a kind of antithesis to the naturalist literature which was popular at the end of the Meiji era. Boldly taking sex as the theme for his novel, he wrote with a symbolist approach, but the sale of the book was prohibited. Deeply moved by the Emperor Meiji's death and the subsequent suicide of General Nogi, Ôgai later wrote *The Last Testament of Okitsu Yagoyemon*, and followed it with several other historical novels. There is a noticeable gap between the very high reputation as a novelist which Ôgai enjoys among the Japanese and the reputation he has among Westerners.

NATSUME SÔSEKI —

Spiritual Anguish in an Age of Modernization

MARIA FLUTSCH

Natsume Sôseki, as one of the great intellects of the Meiji period, is a very interesting figure for Westerners. His deep knowledge of the Chinese classics together with the extensive studies he made in European, especially English, literature made him one of those most highly qualified to judge the values of Western thought as well as its shortcomings.

In *Sorekara* (*And Then* ...) we find Sôseki making very shrewd and keen critical judgements of the Meiji period and its anxiety to modernize. He felt that Japan overrated Western culture and that such indiscriminate copying of the West was wrong and destructive to the soul of Japan.

In the personality of Daisuke, the hero of *Sorekara*, Sôseki attempted to portray the personal problems that every educated Japanese had to face in this age of great change. With technical and material changes Daisuke could cope; with artistic and cultural changes, he could cope. Indeed he enjoyed attending concerts of Western music and art exhibitions.

It was with spiritual values, with the moral and ethical principles from the West, that he had his greatest struggle. A new type of personality had emerged in the West not only with the development of American democratic ideas, with which Sôseki had come into contact through his youthful studies of Walt Whitman, but through the development of British thought as expressed for Sôseki by the English novelists and poets of the period. A strong individualism almost aggressive in its egoism became the highest form of human behaviour. But in Japan the strength of traditional morality and ethics had not waned during this period. They had, in fact, grown stronger as Japan, faced with powerful competition from the West, attempted to compete in the field of international politics. Thus, during this period, not only were the demands upon the personality by the family as strong as ever, but the demands made by society for the sake of the welfare of the country as a whole were a very strong force upon the Meiji person.

In *Sorekara* Sôseki describes the contradictions, the spiritual struggles, the many insoluble problems and sorrows of a man who had to give up his old ideas but was not very eager to accept the new.

This struggle is dramatized in the form of a love story in which Daisuke falls in love with the wife of his best friend and has to make the soul-rending decision whether to follow his own individual happiness and marry her, thus risking the awful censure not only of society but of his own family, who eventually disown him.

But *Sorekara* is not just a philosophical work. Another facet of the Meiji personality can be seen in the beauty of style, in the perfect blending of Western literary principles and Japanese poetic values which Sôseki achieved in *Sorekara*.

For a Westerner who only sees Japan's changes and developments from the outside in terms of material and technological advancement, to read about the mental and spiritual struggles and sufferings that these changes brought about in the hearts of the Meiji Japanese, and are still perhaps bringing about in the hearts of present-day Japanese, is most enlightening.

A study of Sôseki, and especially of *Sorekara*, is essential to the Westerner who wants to understand the Japanese people.

[Note] NATSUME SÔSEKI (1867-1916) went to study in England in 1900. On his return to Japan, he taught English literature at Tokyo Imperial University, and later worked for the Asahi newspaper, concentrating on writing fiction. His talent was recognized with the publication of his first novel, *I Am a Cat*, and he went on to write such novels as *Botchan, Sanshirô* and so forth. *Sorekara* (1909) presents the picture of a young man in the newly developed intellectual elite, suffering from the strain brought on by Japan's modernization process. In this novel Sôseki predicts the fate of the "Japanese Empire," and its later disastrous end. Sôseki is one of the outstanding Japanese novelists of the 20th century and is very widely read even in contemporary Japan.

Shimazaki Tôson —

Before and After the Black Ships

LAWRENCE REDMAN

If asked why I undertook to coordinate a team for the purpose of translating *Yoakemaye* (*Before the Dawn*), my immediate response is to ask, "Why has this not already been made available in English?"

Compare Kawabata's winning the Nobel prize for his novel which deals with the lives of totally useless people in totally pointless circumstances with the fact that Tôson's great life work which deals with the life of a whole nation from its poorest peasant who shakes with fear before his prosecutors, to the Shôgun who lay dying but who called for his formal attire to receive members of his Council of Elders; to all the people high and low, rich and poor, their customs, their fears, their hopes defined by a man who felt a responsibility to make the facts known to history—with the fact that this work has not yet been published in English. Surely a grave dereliction of duty lies here.

Yoakemaye first came to my attention four years ago when a private student of mine showed me a passage she had translated which read: "Spring comes late to the mountains of Kiso, then as the snow melts on the Ina mountain the whole place seemed to come to life . . . ." It was then that I decided that if I were to learn about Japan I ought to do so through the work of a poet, as Tôson seemed then to me to be. I therefore determined to organize a team of translators for that purpose. Apart from the fact that I was later to learn that this was no mean feat, as the language used by Tôson was not always ordinary, not to mention modern, I also discovered that he was very much a humanist. And since I had already, a year or so earlier, written a novel which dealt with the lives of the ordinary people of England faced with the threat of destruction by the Hitlerites, and since I myself have been an armchair politician for very many years, I have felt a great affinity for the man and his work.

Yoakemaye is a historical biography which deals with the emergence of Japan out of the stage of feudalism and into the present stage of capitalism. But that is not all. As is very well known, this stage in Japan's progress took place at a time when Western nations were busily engaged in gobbling up large sectors of the earth's surface in order to bend the peoples and the raw material possessions of those areas to their voracious needs.

The hero of this great masterpiece is Hanzô (the author's father). And it begins with Hanzô as a sensitive and idealistic young fellow, that is to say he has a decided social consciousness—he loves his people quite as much as he loves his country. He is pained at the sight of the misery of the masses as he watches their condition grow daily worse in a miasma of corruption in high places and in low—currency speculation, hoarding, rampant inflation, alliances, re-alliances, intrigues, rumours, plots, assassinations, earthquakes, massive conflagrations, wars, etc. That is to say, as we follow Hanzô and his contemporaries, we follow a history recorded in vivid detail of the life of a whole nation in dire distress and at the point of a mighty social upheaval, seeking urgently for a solution at a time when they were faced with the additional threat from an external force—the Black Ships—(American warships commanded by Commodore Perry who sought to open Japan to U.S. trade).

What I think is the most absorbingly interesting element contained in this great masterpiece is that it tells us in some detail what was happening in Japan at the time of Perry's arrival, and of its consequences. Perry's bullying arrogance, the opening of the Yokohama port, the doubts, the fears, the compromises, the capitulations—how like the world as it stands today!

"The Black Ships! The Black Ships!" That is the leitmotiv to which Tôson returns again and again throughout the opening chapters of his great work. The Black Ships that stood off the Edo (Tokyo) Bay were like a kind of "Sword of Damocles," or, better put in Tôson's words: "The supreme embodiment of the human systematized will and its natural purpose sought out the primitive and noble being in its quest for greedy profit, such were the U.S. Black Ships!"

It was those black ships which paved the way for the currency speculations, the shortages and price rises, the further abject impoverishment of the people to the level of "indescribable misery" as Tôson put it, all of which worked to hasten the downfall of the Shogunate and later—and this Hanzô was not to know—the emergence of the land he loved to the level of a colossus among the mighty nations of the earth.

I together with my good friends, have set to work on the translation of *Yoakemaye* because it is a most honorable undertaking, because it will provide, we believe, a significant contribution to world literature, and because it will contribute to a better international understanding of the Japanese people.

[Note] SHIMAZAKI TÔSON (1872-1943) became well known as a poet while quite young, and his poetry is still enjoyed by many Japanese today. He later published many novels, establishing his reputation as a novelist with *Hakai* (*The Broken Commandment*), the first long novel to depict the tragic situation of Japan's outcast class.

His masterpiece, *Before the Dawn*, was written in 1929. Set in his home village, Kiso, with a central character modelled after Tôson's own father, it is a historical novel which faithfully depicts the rapid changes taking place in Japan immediately before and after the Meiji Restoration.

Ishikawa Takuboku —

Poetry: A Writer's "Sad Toys"

Ruth Linhart

The Japanese poet Ishikawa Takuboku (1886-1912) started his literary career as a *tanka* poet, and it is this literary genre which made him popular in Japan. Yet the poet's attitude towards this literary form was rather ambivalent, and it is one of the tragic aspects of his life that, judging from his letters and diaries, he despised the genre in which he was so gifted.

In his essay *Jidai Heisoku no Genjô* (*The Stagnation of the Times*) he appeals: "What I demand from literature is criticism!" As lyric poetry seemed inappropriate to him as a means for "criticism of our times" and not to answer the need for social reform, he thought little of it. Nevertheless, at the same time, he was emotionally very much inclined towards *tanka* poetry. In his essay *Uta no Iroiro* (*Aspects of the Tanka*) he states: "Tanka are my sad toys." His poems, he explains, are but a means of self-expression, like a diary, "sad" because he wrote them when unhappy, and "sad" because of their uselessness to society. Moreover, there existed a conflict between his goal to become a successful writer of novels, which he could not achieve, and his inconsistent and immature character, which made him more suited for the little form of *tanka*.

This last sentence of *Uta no Iroiro*, "*tanka* are my sad toys" stimulated his friend, the poet, Toki Aika, to call the collection of 194 poems, which was published in 1912 shortly after the death of the 26-year-old Takuboku, *Kanashiki Gangu* (*Sad Toys*). Takuboku had already published a collection of *tanka*, *Ichiaku no Suna* (*A Handful of Sand*) in 1910, many poems of which are among the best-known Japanese *tanka*, but not before *Kanashiki Gangu* did Takuboku find a truly original lyrical expression. While in novels and essays he tried to deal with social problems and his ideas and ideals about society,

Takuboku looks within his own self in *Kanashiki Gangu*. The collection, in describing Takuboku's daily life during the last year before his death, depicts the gradual decay of all human life. Unlike his novels, which he wrote only out of a desire for prestige and money, his *tanka* responded to an emotional need. We read, that "on unhappy days" there was "no greater satisfaction" for him "than to write *tanka*."

As mentioned above, he describes in the poems of *Kanashiki Gangu* his last year of life. This year was marked by his deadly illness of tuberculosis (which also caused his mother's death in the same year, as well as his wife Setsuko's death in 1913), by discord with family and friends, and by severe poverty (he and his family lived at that time exclusively on money borrowed from friends or from the pawnshop). This was also the year of the Kōtoku high treason affair, when a group of anarchists was accused of having plotted to assassinate the Emperor. The incident aroused in Takuboku a strong desire to work for social reform, but he was frustrated by illness and poverty.

This dark background produced *tanka* of a dark, desolate, and nihilistic view of life.

Compared with his first *tanka* collection, *Ichiaku no Suna*, where Takuboku, in a romantic and often sentimental way, wrote of personal reminiscences and events from a dream-world, in *Kanashiki Gangu* we meet a concentration of themes, space and time, persons and emotions, all taken from the desperate circumstances of his everyday life.

When I say,
I believe that a new morning will come,
I do not lie, but . . .

He unmasks and destroys his own hopes and illusions. Accordingly the 194 poems of *Kanashiki Gangu* are a deeply pessimistic, but nevertheless cool and objective description of Takuboku's last phase of life, a very moving autobiography as well as a work of high artistic value. In these tanka, which Takuboku wrote so easily and to which he attached so little value, he created lyrics of metrical and stylistic perfection that made him famous in Japan and touched the hearts of people everywhere.

[Note] *Sad Toys* is the title of the second collection of *tanka* poetry written by ISHIKAWA TAKUBOKU (1886-1912). Takuboku spent his life in poverty, holding many jobs, such as substitute teacher in a primary school, newspaper reporter, etc., until his death at the age of twenty-six. He was always hoping to become a novelist, but this dream was never realized. *Sad Toys* was published by his friend, Toki Zenmaro (Aika), after his death. It has become one of the best known collections of poetry among modern Japanese readers. Takuboku has the reputation of being the greatest writer of traditional Japanese poetry since the Meiji era.

NISHIDA KITARÔ—

A Metaphysical Philosophy of Life

RICHARD WOOD

Nishida Kitarô is often called, "The Representative Philosopher of Japan," a title which makes many Japanese philosophers bristle. There are good reasons for both the title and the objection to it. Contemporary Japanese philosophers who object to regarding Nishida as representative of Japanese philosophy have a point, for the range of philosophical views in Japan is as wide as in any country, maybe even wider because the diversity of influences is wider. Yet, even admitting this point, a case can be made for giving Nishida special recognition in Japanese philosophy. He was the first Japanese philosopher influential enough that a "school" of philosophy came to be based on his ideas. His thought remains something which most Japanese philosophers feel constrained to take seriously, even if they disagree with it. Nishida's philosophy is one of the most interesting and suggestive attempts yet made to unite some main themes and approaches of Western philosophy with some traditional Japanese ideas, especially those of Rinzai Zen Buddhism.

However, to call Nishida a Zen philosopher is too simple, for he never saw his task as the philosophical articulation of Zen Buddhism. Moreover, his work shows profound influence from Christianity, Confucianism, and especially toward the end of his life, from the "other power" idea of the Pure Land Buddhist thought of Hônen and Shinran.

While there is no single key to a philosophy as complex as Nishida's, one theme that runs throughout his works, even the most abstruse and metaphysical, is his concern to account for the moral life. His is always a philosophy of life, of human life in its intellectual, aesthetic, and moral dimensions. Even such apparently remote ideas as "pure experience," "logic of place," and "absolute nothingness" are not far removed from Nishida's humanistic, especially ethical, concerns. To see how the concern for a philosophy of life permeates these metaphysical ideas is to have a good start toward understanding Nishida.

Much of Nishida's later writing is a development and articulation of ideas sketched in his first (and most famous) book, *Zen no Kenkyū* (*A Study of Good*, 1911). While a great deal has been said about the idea of "pure experience" in that work, the theme which shapes not only that idea but its subsequent development into a "logic of place" is the ethical notion that sincerity, which is the deepest demand of the personality, is at the same time the loss of self-consciousness and the fusion of the self with the other. "Only when subject and object are mutually submerged, the thing and the self are mutually forgotten, and one arrives at a state wherein there is only the activity of a single reality in heaven and earth, does one first attain to the consummation of good behavior." (*A Study of Good*, trans. by Viglielmo, p. 145)

This theme persists throughout Nishida's thought. In *A Study of Good* itself, "pure experience" as the condition of consciousness in which there is yet neither subject nor object, is the metaphysical theory underlying this ethical theme. Through his later idea of a "logic of place" (the place of nothingness in which absolute free will expresses itself), Nishida eliminates the psychologistic elements of "pure experience," while keeping the core notion that the ultimate perfection of self is at once absolute self-determination and complete loss of self-consciousness. The schema for this development is already present in *A Study of Good*: The only intrinsic good is fulfillment of the deepest demands of personality. Since personality is individual, the ultimate good is found in full development of individuality. Yet individuality has a social base; in fact it is best understood as drawing out various dimensions of that social base. But from a wider perspective, the social base is not something given, nor something ultimate (a point relevant to the nationalism controversy), but is nothing more than the self-expression of personality (will). The idea of "absolute nothingness" is a symbol for the recognition that the development of personality (of will) rests upon no foundation beyond itself.

An application of this schema can be seen in Nishida's interpretation of Japanese culture in two late works, *Fundamental Problems of Philosophy* and *The Problem of Japanese Culture.* He sees classical Japanese culture as based on the affirmation of absolute nothingness, on the subordination of space to time, of intellect to feeling. He again stresses the theme that complete responsiveness to the world, or real empathy with another, requires loss of self-consciousness. "Absolute nothingness" becomes the term around which a systematic treatment of this insight is attempted.

Nishida's insistence on the ultimate unity of self and other, of self and world, provided him with a solid philosophical base to resist the excessive nationalism of the 1930's. Even under pressure, his view remained fundamentally cosmopolitan. On the other side his resistance to a "lowest common denominator" approach to the philosophy of culture, his stress on the potential of each individual and each cultural tradition to add to the richness of an ideal universal culture, is a strikingly contemporary note.

[Note] NISHIDA KITARÔ (1870-1945) did not have a very distinguished academic background graduating from a normal school, but as a result of his own reading and study of Zen he wrote *A Study of Good*. This book is highly valued as the first original philosophical work produced by a modern Japanese writer, and it is still widely read. Nishida wrote in his diary: "I am neither a psychologist nor a sociologist. I simply want to be a student of *life*." This shows his fundamental approach to his research. Eventually, despite his undistinguished school education, he was invited to become a full professor at Kyoto Imperial University, one of the two highest peaks in the Japanese academic world, where he developed a philosophical system known as "Nishida philosophy." The followers of Nishida came to be called the "Nishida school." His close friend Suzuki Daisetsu reminisced about Nishida with these words: "He was not a philosopher who did nothing but speculate. He was warm-hearted and full of life."

NAGAI KAFÛ—

The Death of the Arts of Edo

DONALD RICHIE

Nagai Kafû wanted to be buried among the courtesans of the Yoshiwara.[1] Family pride and the traditional Japanese sense of fitness prevailed, however, and he is buried instead in respectable Zôshigaya.

He wanted to be buried in Yoshiwara not only because he knew and loved the area, as he later loved Tamanoi,[2] and as he had always loved Asakusa,[3] but because here he found all that was left alive of old Tokyo.

The flavor of old Edo lingered when he was young. Later he sought the last of the old Meiji feeling in the capital. Still later, after the war, he sought out all that was left of old Taishô atmosphere. It does not matter that he hated the Meiji and Taishô periods when he was living during them. What he was searching for was not only the past. He was also searching for a vitality in Tokyo, the only city—perhaps the only thing—he ever loved.

He explains this feeling in the *Edo Geijutsuron* (*Essays on the Arts of Edo*) when, in talking of the *ukiyoye* he explains: "It induces in me feelings almost religious. *Ukiyoye* was the special art form of the oppressed Edo plebeian, created in the face of constant harassment. The Kanô line, or the Academy of the eighteenth century, which had the protection of the government, failed to pass on to us the true artistic glories of its day. That task was performed instead by the despised artist of the town, virtually in shackles, even threatened with banishment. Is not *ukiyoye* the triumphal song of the common man who refused to bow down?"

It is this feeling for living vitality which enabled Kafû to love the *yose, rakugo, manzai*,[4] and the common skit of the Asakusa music hall. His heroines all share this vitality, from O-nami in *Yume no*

Onna (*The Dream Woman*) through O-yuki in *Bokutô Kidan* (*A Strange Tale from East of the River*). These are common girls who refused to bow down.

In the end, of course, authority always wins. It was the Kanô line, as it were, that put Kafû in the Zôshigaya cemetery. It is the Kanô line that, even now, prevents a full publication of his work. It is the Kanô line that quibbles about Kafû's supposed pornography, and harasses those who would publish it.

Today we see the Kanô line triumphant. Flower-arranging, tea ceremony, etc., all are packaged and presented as the only Japanese culture. All are imported to the shores of credulous and interested foreigners. No one would now suspect that there was also another culture in Japan, one much older and much more vital. The *yose* are closed and the artists forced to dilute themselves on television, the Yoshiwara is dark, Tamanoi is now a fairly respectable residential district, Asakusa has again become a country town, and Uyeno is now only a railway terminal.

The Kanô line is beautiful, austere, technically superb, but it is not vital. It was fit for the museum from the beginning, it was always in very good taste. It was never alive in the way, however, that Kafû understood the term.

He declared early in his career, in the epilogue to *Jigoku no Hana* (*The Flowers of Hell*) that he would write about the "darker side," the "naked force." Accepting this "darker side," this "naked force," means accepting both the Japanese and man in general as he really is. It is this "naked force" that is missing in the Kanô line and which the Japanese have now successfully erased from their art.

Politically, the Kanô line is the same thing as the Tokugawa government. In contemporary Japan one may say that the Tokugawa *bakufu* has, finally, had complete success. Except for Kafû and a few others like him. They seem to remember some pre-Tokugawa time when people were still whole. And I believe there was such a time, before the dead hand of the Tokugawa government rested so heavily on the Japanese people. I search for it myself.

Therefore I feel very close to Kafû. But does anyone read Kafû any more? He is a "literary classic," I know, but this usually means no one enjoys the writer any more. The West is more fortunate. He is well translated and there is one excellent book about him: *Kafû the Scribbler*, by Edward Seidensticker (Stanford University Press, Stanford, California, 1965).

But, in a way, it makes no difference if he is read. 1959 is the year he died and that is also the year for the beginning of Japan's new prosperity, for its so-called leisure boom, and for the ultimate triumph of the Kanô line. Kafû, living (until 1945) in his Henkikan house, seemed to know this. I, now living in my Tsukiji house in 1974, know this. The old way—the way of the *yose* and of Tamanoi—is gone. Yet, I, like Kafû, would like to continue to celebrate it.

[Note] NAGAI KAFÛ (1879-1959) disliked studies from the time he was in high school, and made up his mind to become a novelist. His father wanted him to become a businessman and sent him to study in America, but he developed a great enthusiasm for French literature, and began to have increased contacts with prostitutes. Kafû studied in France for a while, then returned to Japan and soon after wrote *Stories from America*. His reputation as a writer began to grow, and he published several more works of fiction. Soon he was invited to become full professor at Keiô University. He took an esthetic approach to fiction, in opposition to the naturalist movement, and his works usually dealt with the lower class prostitutes whom he was partial to. One of his best works, *A Strange Tale from East of the River*, depicts the world of these women. In his later years he wrote little that was noteworthy, and led a lonely life, keeping people at a distance except for friendly chorus girls from the Asakusa theater district. One of the reasons for his turning his back on ordinary society and living the way he did was said to be the Kôtoku high treason case. (see p. 35)
1. 2. Tokyo's red-light districts. 3. Old-fashioned entertainment district. 4. Plebeian entertainments.

TANIZAKI JUN'ICHIRÔ —

The Aesthetics of Daily Life in Japan

NORMAN H. TOLMAN

Although many Japanese are well versed in foreign languages, those who are not, and who wish to read the literature of almost any other country, need only to rush off to one of the 8,654 bookstores in Japan. In most cases, they will find what they are seeking—available in the Japanese language.

The level of translation here is among the best in the world. One company alone translates and publishes a book every other day of the year.

For the foreigner the situation is very different. The number of foreigners who can read Japanese literature in the original is very restricted, and therefore we *must* rely mainly on translations. However, in the case of Japanese literature in translation, a sad state of affairs exists. Every year there are more books translated (some 2,000) from English into Japanese than there have been translated from Japanese into English in all history.

The result is that it would be possible in one college year to read a major portion of the Japanese literature that has been translated into English. Unfortunately, a great many outstanding Japanese authors, masters of their language and skilled storytellers, never find their way into print in other languages.

One of those who has is Tanizaki Jun'ichirô, many of whose works have been translated into English. Perhaps his best known book, both in Japan and abroad, is *The Makioka Sisters*, or *Sasame Yuki* as it is known in the original Japanese. Even from the very beginning we can see the problems of the translator—"thin snow" means nothing in English and conveys no image, so the translator is forced to give the book a new title.

As this title tells us, the story is about sisters, four of them, and the kind of life they lived in Osaka during the period just before the war from 1936 to 1941. Tanizaki wrote the book in 1947 when he was over sixty and had lived through the war and the bitter days after it. It seems generally accepted that writing this story must have been a way for him (and for his Japanese readers) to re-live some of the pleasant memories of the good old days that seemed as though they would never come again.

For Western readers the book is of value for quite different reasons. It captures with almost unbelievable detail and accuracy an era which few foreigners could know, and it provides a picture of daily life in Japan which I have never found in any other book.

Even today, Westerners have almost no conception of the daily happenings of Japanese life. Most Japanese automatically, without thinking, slip off their shoes before entering a room; this action is so much a part of life that they never think to write about it. In cases of this sort, Tanizaki writes with a fascination for the scene, almost as if he were not Japanese himself. He has paid such careful attention to the daily doings that most people just take for granted and never notice. The result is that even the novice to Japanese culture feels as though he has learned a great deal about what goes on in Japan when he puts the book down, and feels that if he ever happened to meet one of the Makioka sisters he would know her quite well.

Although this book has been criticized by Western experts on Japanese literature as being weak in plot, it is exactly this point that makes it of particular interest to me. When the reader is finished he is left with a memory of a series of almost unrelated incidents, some of incredible beauty because they are so "Japanese." Who but Tanizaki would so meticulously describe o-miai[1] meetings and cherry blossom viewing. To Westerners who have developed neither of these things to the point of being such refined rituals as they are in Japan, when first encountered in Tanizaki's *Sasame Yuki*, they become memories that last forever.

I first read this book in translation in a course on Japanese literature at Yale University. It was a time when I knew very little about Japan. I found the book to be irresistible and have regretted to this day that although I was fortunate during my diplomatic career in meeting many outstanding Japanese, including many authors like Kawabata and Mishima, I was never able to meet and discuss this book, which still holds a place in my heart as one of my favorites, with the great Tanizaki.

[Note] TANIZAKI JUN'ICHIRÔ (1886-1965) first won recognition in 1910, with the publication of his short story *Tattoo*. His estheticism and art-for-art's-sake approach to literature stood in opposition to the naturalist movement which was then dominant in Japan. Later he began to draw many of his materials from the Japanese classics, and wrote some outstanding works such as *Ashikari, A Portrait of Shunkin*, and *A Cat, Shôzô, and Two Women*.

The Makioka Sisters was begun in 1943, in the middle of the Second World War, and completed after the war. Centering around four sisters from a wealthy merchant family in Osaka, the story presents a type of the pre-war Japanese family and at the same time meticulously depicts the background of the prewar period. Reading the novel is like watching the unfolding of a Japanese picture scroll.

Tanizaki continued to write prolifically until the last years of his life, when he wrote *Kagi* (*The Key*) and other such works that he called "an old man's literature." He is regarded as one of the greatest of modern Japanese writers, and his work is well known throughout the world.

1. In Japan, parents, relatives, and family friends help young men and women find their spouse. An *o-miai* is usually held at a restaurant or theater, when a young man and a young woman are introduced to each other in the presence of their families. If they like each other, they begin dating. It may or may not lead to their marriage since it is entirely up to the two to decide.

Akutagawa Ryûnosuke —

Perfection in Form and Style

Beverley D. Tucker

My first impression of Akutagawa Ryûnosuke was through the movie *Rashômon*, which I saw in Washington in 1952. I was fascinated and impressed, but also puzzled. Not long after that a Japanese friend gave me a copy of *Kappa*, translated into English by his former teacher, telling me it was something like *Gulliver's Travels*. At that time, having very little knowledge of Japan for a background, I was again puzzled, although I found the book interesting.

But my next exposure to Akutagawa was direct and, for me, very important. This was when I read *Kumo no Ito* (*The Spider's Thread*) in one of the Naganuma Readers, which, like so many other foreigners, I labored through to study the Japanese language. It was in reading this story that, for the first time, I was able to feel real aesthetic appreciation of something read in Japanese.

This experience made me think that Akutagawa's genius must indeed have been great, if even an ignorant foreigner like myself could catch a glimpse of that beauty.

Since then I have read a good deal more. I would not be telling the truth, however, if I said that my admiration for Akutagawa has continued to grow. Something of that same beauty I found in others of his short stories, but I cannot say that I found any of them more beautiful. Nor have I found their intellectual content or their ideas necessarily more profound.

When I read of Akutagawa's life, his mother's madness and early death, his adoption in another family, and his poor health and fear of his own mental breakdown, I could not but feel sympathy for this spiritually tortured writer. In this respect there are many similarities between him and Edgar Allan Poe. Poe's mother died when he was not yet three, and like Akutagawa, he was brought up in another family, the Allans, although he was never formally adopted. Both writers were acutely sensitive to sensual stimulation, and it seems clear that Akutagawa was influenced by Poe's theories of art and beauty as expressed in *The Poetic Principle* and elsewhere. Like Poe before him, Akutagawa thought that art provided the only thing of lasting and transcending value in this evil and ephemeral world. For this reason form and style were all-important, and each work had to be polished and made perfect.

Akutagawa followed Poe's dictum that every word must contribute to "a certain single effect," and perhaps for this reason neither writer was able to sustain the self-imposed unity to create long works. Both excelled in the short story and characteristically portrayed moods of horror, melancholy, hatred, and despair. There are many parallels. For instance, the consuming passion of the artist Yoshihide in *Hell Screen (Jigokuhen)*, who produces a masterpiece at the sacrifice of the model, is an echo of Poe's *The Oval Portrait*; but in this case Akutagawa's is by far the greater work. It was their morbid self-consciousness which enabled both writers to penetrate into psychological regions usually hidden to others.

Like Poe, Akutagawa was fascinated by the supernatural, and it is significant that one of his longer works, *Kappa*, deals almost entirely with a world of creatures in the supernatural world of Japanese folklore. The protagonist is, like many of Poe's heroes, partly mad, but sane enough to make the supernatural seem as real as everyday life. There is no question but that Akutagawa was conscious of Swift's work. The entrance into *Kappaland* is also similar to *Alice in Wonderland*. Nevertheless, these are only details of the framework, and *Kappa* is a highly original creation which attests to the power of Akutagawa's imagination. He may have used ideas found in Western writers, just as he used stories from the ancient tales of China and Japan, or as Shakespeare and other writers used the history and literature of Greece and Rome, but he made them unmistakably his own.

Kappa was written in February 1927, only about five months before his suicide on July 24 of that year, at a time when he was harassed by his own poor health, the suicide of his brother-in-law in January, and by feelings of paranoia which had been increasing for several years. All these things give to *Kappa* a negative quality, a turning away from life. Like the unborn Kappa, Akutagawa seems to be saying, "I maintain that . . . . existence is evil." In Swift there is scathing criticism, but usually a positive purpose. In *Kappa* there is no indication that Akutagawa hoped for improvement. And yet it is a mark of his genius that there are bright touches of humor, and the book with all its negative aspects can still be read with enjoyment, if not delight. Circumstances and his own poor health, both physical and mental, prevented Akutagawa from writing the great works which we expect from great writers, but the perfection of some of his short stories gives him a place among those who have been granted the gift of communicating glimpses of lasting beauty through their art.

[Note] AKUTAGAWA RYÛNOSUKE (1892-1927) was adopted as a small child by the Akutagawa family after his own mother went insane. This early experience left him emotionally scarred for the rest of his life, and influenced the character of his writing. He is recognized as an outstanding short story writer in Japan. In his early works he drew much material from classical literature. Stories such as the one made famous in the film *Rashômon* were based on the *Konjaku Monogatari*.

After he passed the age of thirty his health began to decline, and a melancholy tone began to be predominant in his writing. Five months after writing *Kappa*, presented as the narration of the experiences of an insane man, he committed suicide. *Kappa*, a comic novel satirizing human society, takes its name from an imaginary animal believed by the Japanese to live at the water's edge.

Tokuda Shûsei —

A Novelist with No Secrets

Robert Rolf

Despite the great bulk of fiction that Tokuda Shûsei produced during his long writing career that stretched from the 1890's to World War II, only a few of his stories have been translated in Western languages. Fortunately, however, one of these is the short story *Kunshô* (1935), which has been translated into English, German, and Hungarian. For readers of English it is easily accessible in the Ivan Morris translation, *Order of the White Paulownia*, found in his *Modern Japanese Stories: An Anthology*.

Order of the White Paulownia is a memorable story, of interest not only for its intrinsic qualities but also for what it leads one to expect from Shûsei's other important fictions. Shûsei is noted for his many moving fictional portraits of women, usually city girls from the lower classes struggling to cope with unsympathetic husbands or patrons. In *Order of the White Paulownia* the woman is Kanako, a highly believable heroine who is married off to a fast-living veteran of military service in Manchuria. Originally she was to marry a milder, more pleasant fellow, but his relatives substituted the ex-soldier almost at the last moment in the hope that marriage would halt his compulsive gambling and general irresponsibility. *Order of the White Paulownia* chronicles Kanako's difficulties in managing married life with her hopeless husband and with no sympathy from either her in-laws or her own family. Traditionally a woman in Japan is expected to resign herself to her fate, so that her complaints about her husband's excesses are interpreted as selfish by her relatives.

Shûsei's work is often characterized as gloomy, but a reading of *Order of the White Paulownia* will show that his gloom is neither excessive nor unwarranted. Shûsei was a man of the people; he considered himself just a common man and did not pretend to the

rarefied air of more "serious" novelists. He was a notorious woman-
izer, who shocked his literary colleagues through his open affairs with
young women, and who even helped establish an ex-mistress as the
proprietress of a *geisha* house. The authoress Hayashi Fumiko once
characterized Shûsei as a man with no secrets, who was equally at
home whether with his sleeves pulled up and doing the accounts on
an abacus for his lady friend at her *geisha* house or giving a speech at
the P.E.N. Club. Shûsei is known as a clear-sighted observer of Japanese life, and this perception combines with his unaffected naturalness to give his fiction a raw vitality lacking in the works of many
more well-known Japanese writers.

The influence of Zola is often mentioned when discussing Shûsei,
for he first attained literary prominence in company with other
members of the Zola-influenced Japanese naturalist movement with
the appearance of *A New Home (Arajotai)* in 1908. Their works are
quite different, however. In works like the novella *Arajotai*, for
example, Shûsei never attempts the fictional scope of Zola's novels.
A New Home concerns the marriage of a young, hard-working
shopkeeper and his inability to communicate with his young bride.
They are basically incompatible, but within the social context of
Meiji Japan they must put the fulfillment of their roles as husband
and wife above their personal contentment. They are human beings
and they instinctively crave happiness nonetheless, so that when
another woman enters the picture their marriage seems doomed.

The intense focus upon the psychology of a few characters in *A
New Home* and many of Shûsei's other major works enables him to
achieve a depth of characterization not possible in many of Zola's
novels of greater length. Although Shûsei does not re-create a whole
society, as Zola does wonderfully in such masterpieces as *L'Assommoir,
Nana,* and *Germinal,* Shûsei is, as hinted by the title of his last work,
the unfinished *Miniature (Shukuzu,* 1941), a master of the miniature.
In *Arajotai* Shinkichi and his wife Saku, while comparatively sub-
dued, remind one more of similar troubled married couples by American naturalist writers, like Trina and McTeague in *McTeague* by
Frank Norris (1899) and Carrie and Hurstwood in *Sister Carrie* by

Theodore Dreiser (1900), than of Zola.

If time and the translators are kind to Shûsei, someday he too will undoubtedly take his place among the significant naturalist writers of the world.

[Note] TOKUDA SHÛSEI (1871-1943) published his first novel at the age of twenty, but his down-to-earth style met with little approval in those days when romantic literature predominated. He was not fully recognized as a novelist until the end of the Meiji era, when he was about forty years old. At that time naturalist fiction was flourishing, and Tokuda can be numbered as one of the writers of that school. When he was about fifty he became involved in a scandalous love affair which he turned into material for a confessional novel. This technique of revealing one's own private life with practically no fiction added, attempting to strike a common chord of interest and sympathy with the reader, was one of the conspicuous innovations introduced by Japan's naturalist literature. Toward the end of his life Tokuda was writing his masterpiece, a long work entitled *Miniature*, with a prostitute as the central character, but the military authorities intervened and prevented him from completing it.

Shiga Naoya —

God of the Written Word

ANDRÉ BRUNET

Shiga Naoya is not well-known abroad, as are Mori Ôgai and Natsume Sôseki who lived before him or Akutagawa Ryûnosuke and Tanizaki Jun'ichirô after him. But he does occupy an important place in the history of Japanese literature, both for his influence on other authors and for his unique style.

Born in 1883 near Sendai, Shiga Naoya left Tokyo Imperial University without finishing his studies, and with some of his friends, among them Mushanokôji Saneatsu, founded a literary review called *Shirakaba* (*White Birch*). This magazine marked a reaction against the naturalist school and advocated a more individualistic expression, through which the writer could better communicate his emotions to the reader. It is of interest to note that the proponents of this new school had great admiration for the French post-impressionists and fauves, particularly Cézanne, Van Gogh, Gauguin, and Matisse. That these painters were themselves to some extent influenced by the Japanese woodblock prints suggests that, though perhaps unaware of the fact, the *Shirakaba* authors were indirectly connected with the pictorial art of their own country.

Shiga Naoya did not invent the literary genre of short stories for which he became famous, but he brought this form to a degree of perfection that has never been excelled since. And he developed and expanded the "I novel," of which examples existed before him, but to which he imparted a quality that was never surpassed in later years by his many imitators.

In contrast with the conflict between East and West often found in other authors' works, Shiga Naoya is concerned only with the purely Japanese sensibility, ignoring problems that arise from contact with European or American novels. His pointillist style, bent on noting the minute details of his environment and of his experiences, was at its best in short stories that often verge on essays. Thus, it is hardly surprising that he wrote only one novel, but of such proportions that it took him two-thirds of his long life to finish. In this work, *An'ya Kôro* (*Journey in Darkness*), he embodied part of his own unhappy childhood in an attempt to prove that only in a union with nature can true peace of mind be found.

Perhaps more than for any other of his claims to fame, Shiga Naoya will be remembered for his exemplary style. It is with good reason that he was called *"bunshô no kamisama"* (*"God of the written word"*). His sensitive, but at the same time shy humanism is expressed in sentences of exceptional beauty, where words look like so many gems that blend into a piece of translucid and fascinating crystal. Any foreigner seeking a model for his own Japanese compositions should take Shiga Naoya as an example, impossible to imitate, but eminently worthy as an ultimate goal.

[Note] SHIGA NAOYA (1883-1971) belonged to the "White Birch" school of novelists, who took their name from the magazine which they published, *Shirakaba* (*White Birch*). All of them came from an upper class background, and all except Arishima Takeo (who committed suicide with a married woman when he was forty-five) lived long lives. Because Shiga began his career early and soon brought his style to perfection, he was regarded while still young as a "master" and an example for later writers either to follow or to react against.

Kawabata Yasunari —

The Mystery of Japanese Space

Philippe Robert

The works of Kawabata have been well-received in the West. Among them, *Thousand Cranes* is regarded as "very Japanese;" but I wonder if this impression is not based upon the contrast the novel offers to modern Japanese life. I should like to set down here some personal reflections arising from my reading of *Thousand Cranes*.

What, I wondered, could I pick out from that delicate and sensual atmosphere without destroying the harmonious unity that enveloped the entire work? Then, it arose, I know not from where—the memory, more insistent than ever, of the objects in the novel. Of course, objects play a part in all communications between people, but Kawabata seems to have used them to propel the action of the novel, somewhat in the manner of a photographer. The little utensils used in the tea ceremony are in fact vehicles of meaning. Having a long history, they possess their own destinies.

In *Thousand Cranes* objects, through the symbolic power with which they are invested, become as third persons. They serve as intermediaries in communications between people, but are also "active" — they embody the will of all those who have ever used them. Living people try to express their wishes through spiritualized objects — objects endowed with will. Therein lies the mystery of Japanese space.

Thousand Cranes is not, properly speaking, a novel of action. Yet there is a progression of profundity, if not of plot. The more fully the affinity between things is revealed, the more inexplicable become the motives of human actions. Objects are not only integrated into the space in which the characters evolve, but also cannot be disassociated from it.

Naturally, it is always woman who is most receptive to this profound world of mysterious affinities, particularly the young woman. Fumiko, in a burst of extreme devotion that goes beyond reasoned thought, gives an object. The letter that she writes to Kikuji does not seem very important, but the value she attaches to it suggests a much greater significance than may be apparent. In her child-like simplicity, shocked by her mother's weakness, she is impelled to disqualify herself from society. Thus there is forced upon her the comparison with Inamura Yukiko, which she expresses symbolically through the comparison of her mother's everyday tea bowl with bowls that are works of art. She decides to kill herself—to "break the tea bowl." That must have been what she wrote in her letter. And, strangely, her meeting with Kikuji partakes of the same purity of feeling as did her resolution not to see him. How much meaning there is in Kikuji's attitude, when "he did not pick up the little cup for a long time, preferring to gaze upon it."

(Tr. by Janine Beichman)

[Note] KAWABATA YASUNARI (1899-1972) was still very young when his parents and grandparents died, leaving him an orphan. His subsequent loneliness combined with a weak physical constitution cast a delicate shadow over all his writing. His talent as a novelist was first recognized with the publication of *Izu no Odoriko* (*The Izu Dancer*) in 1926, and his reputation was firmly established with the appearance of *Yukiguni* (*The Snow Country*) in 1935. *Senbazuru* (*Thousand Cranes*) and *Yama no Oto* (*The Sound of the Mountain*), written after the Second World War, deal with completely ordinary everyday events, but capture with fine perception the vague feelings deep in the human subconscious, presenting them in an almost casual manner. The inattentive reader may find nothing of significance in these books, but the sensitive reader is chilled by the discovery of the strangeness hidden in the depths of the human heart, as seen under the author's cool gaze. The traditional sense of beauty in the Japanese classics is perhaps better preserved in the novels of Kawabata than of any other writer. In 1968 he received the Nobel Prize for literature, and four years later, for reasons unknown, he committed suicide.

WATSUJI TETSURÔ—

Climate, Culture, and Human Nature

JUAN MASIA

It was toward the end of my second year in Japan that I read Watsuji's *Fûdo* for the first time. When I was talking with my Japanese teacher about the difficulty of adjusting to the climate of this country, he recommended the book to me. After finishing the third chapter I felt that the author's reflections upon his European experiences had much in common with my own puzzlement as a Westerner challenged by Japanese culture.

I was especially interested in the chapter which dealt with the Japanese national character. Indeed, reading this work taught me much about the culture and the people I was trying so hard to understand. I felt I could find in the events of my daily life in Japan the best proof of what Watsuji says about the "typhonic nature" of the Japanese people, their rapid shifts from one emotion to another, their sensitiveness, the peculiar nature of human relations among them, and the amazing number of contradictions in their ways of thinking.

Also, in an indirect way, Watsuji's ideas helped me to see the Western world from a new viewpoint. While reading his description of Italy and Greece I would try to see the Mediterranean environment as seen through Japanese eyes. Moreover, Watsuji's considerations gave me insights into my own country, even though he does not specifically describe the climate and culture of Spain. What he says of the contrast between the rainy season in the Far East, the dryness of the Arabian desert, and the smoothness of the green Italian fields made me think of the different nuances of climate one can find within such a small zone as the Iberian peninsula. I should have liked to invite Watsuji to travel from the desertic wilderness of Castilla into the green meadows of the northern coast of Spain or into the fruit gardens of Valencia.

Much more profound than these climatic considerations were Watsuji's thoughts on the relation between the peculiarity of a culture and the universality of human nature. When I was correcting the proofs of my Spanish translation of *Fûdo* I happened also to be checking the Japanese translation of Unamuno's *The Essence of Spain*. Both Watsuji and Unamuno (1864-1936) were confronted with the tension between "native culture" and "imported culture." Since I was familiar with Unamuno's ideas on the mutual complementarity of the world's different cultures I was happy to find a similar way of thinking in the following words of Watsuji:

> The man with the best sense of hearing recognizes musical talent best of all; and the one with the finest physique recognizes athletic prowess more readily than any other ... So too the bearer of reason shines most brightly in a meadow climate, and in the monsoon zone the refinement of "feeling" is best recognized. And so, just as we make music our own through the musician, or are able to experience a game through an athlete, might we not learn to cultivate our reason from the place where the light of reason shines the brightest, and to perfect the refinement of our feelings with the help of places where refinement of feeling is best re-alized?

This idea of an enriching encounter between different cultures is colorfully expressed by Watsuji through the image of the Japanese bamboo covered with snow. The Spanish reader, of course, will need an explanation to grasp this image. For him, the tropical atmosphere evoked by the bamboo does not go together with a landscape of snow. But, once the context is understood, the image of the Japanese bamboo bending under the weight of the snow suggests a synthesis of climatic characteristics which might have seemed, at first sight, irrec-oncilable. We are encouraged to remain deeply rooted in our own culture, and yet to be open enough to transcend it.

[Note] WATSUJI TETSURÔ (1889-1960) was a professor of philosophy at Tokyo Imperial University. He first attracted attention for his studies of

Nietzsche and Kierkegaard. Later his interests turned to the study of Japanese culture as well as of the origins of Buddhism and Christianity. On the basis of these studies he attempted to formulate a view of Japanese ethical thought within an international context.

Fûdo (*Climate and Culture*), the title of his best-known work, is a word denoting the peculiar characteristics of a geographical region, which comprehends not only the natural features of that region, but the influence of nature upon the people of the region as well. Watsuji wrote *Fûdo* as a macroscopic study of the different *fûdo* of the world, using the instance of Japan to analyze the relationship between the natural features of a given region and the culture created by the people living there.

Dazai Osamu —

The Disintegration of Personality in Modern Man

Čiháková Vlasta

Literature is becoming more the expression of man's revolt against modern society, and less the depiction of his romantic vision. And yet it remains the only objective expression of his personal experience, his soul's confessions. Ultimately authenticity itself will become the principal aim of all creation. Probably this trend is related to the more general problem of the bifurcation of man's personality in modern society, where personal behavior is no longer considered inseparable from social behavior. Literature comes to stand in opposition to society, as the expression of spiritual revolt in man's struggle to preserve his integrity as a human being. Thus the works of Dostoevski and Solzhenitsyn, or Camus and Samuel Lewis, despite their different historical and social contexts, formulate man's common ideals—self-realization as the highest value in human action, and freedom of will and sensibility as the highest ethical criteria.

However, the most beautiful literature does not present solutions to these fundamental problems, but seeks only an eloquent way of putting the questions. If they are put in a personal, intimate way, they will appeal to both senses and reason. Every major work of modern literature has a certain intimacy. This has nothing to do with traditional esthetic or ethical norms, or with whether the work is "polished" or "rough." Rather it is the intimacy of the deepest dimension of man's experience in an age that has lost its God, when old, established values are disintegrating. The Japanese author who best expresses this intimacy with the soul of modern man is Dazai Osamu.

"At New Year's time I received a *kimono*. It was a gift. The material was hemp, woven in soft gray stripes—a summer *kimono*. 'To live until summer . . . ,' I thought." Thus begins his novel *Last Years*

(*Bannen*). What delicacy and sensitivity of expression! This is the quality for which Dazai is so much admired by the young and those who are up-to-date. Some adults, however, care little for his writing. They cannot bear the intimacy of his language—just as many of them cannot tolerate the existence of homosexuals. But Dazai's subjectivity is of a complicated sort, having its origins in the complex structure of the Japanese way of thinking. He divides society into the "weak" and the "strong." He himself was one of the "weak," of course, because for him the "strong" lacked all sensitivity. In *Ningen Shikkaku* (*No Longer Human*) he wrote:

"For me the most incomprehensible people are those who deceive each other daily, and yet have the confidence to go through life cheerfully, happily, and in good spirits."

Yet on the other hand he knew that society was controlled and manipulated by the "strong," and so he could not refuse to communicate and associate with them.

He tried to bridge the gap with his "drollery." But the tragedy of Dazai's life is that he could never find any other form of human contact with the "strong." "People live quite coolly in mutual distrust, without any dependence upon Jehovah or anything else—don't they?" he wrote in the same novel. He deplored the loss of Christian beliefs, and yet was not so naive as to conceive new ethical values within the formalistic structure of Japanese society, which had been deprived of all warmth by modern civilization. He sought his solution within himself. He lived the absurd, paradoxical life of an Ivan Karamazov, creating Christ—or Anti-Christ—within himself. This served well enough to integrate his own being, yet the isolation of such absolute freedom forced him ultimately to take his own life. In this final demonstration of personal freedom, as well as in the intimacy of the situations he treats in his work, his highest value seems to lie in the "drollery" that bridges the gap between "weak" and "strong."

[Note] DAZAI OSAMU (1909-1948), like many Japanese intellectuals of his time, became involved in communist activities while he was a student, and all his life had a feeling of guilt for having deserted the movement. He attempted suicide twice and failed. Defeated in life, he adopted the literary stance of a laughing, masochistic clown, and this gave his writing a freshness which soon brought him recognition. After the Second World War his novels had wide appeal for the unsettled people living in the confused Japanese society of that time, and he became a very popular writer. But at the height of his popularity he attempted suicide for the third time (a double suicide with a woman), and this time was successful. He is idolized even today, and his novels are widely read, especially by young people who are fond of literature.

Ibuse Masuji—

In Search of the Wellsprings of Language and Imagination
Anthony V. Limán

The other day I sat down with a little friend of mine and we leafed through his encyclopedia.

I said: "This must be a *tonbo*[1] and this a *yanma*[2]."

"No. Animals," said he, very firmly. I turned the page and tried again.

"Isn't this a *monshirochô*[3] and this a *monkichô*[4]?

"No. Insects," concluded the boy. I gave up and agreed that a bee is a fly, a wasp is a fly and—thank God—a fly is a fly.

Someday I would like to take the boy on a fishing trip. We would take a back-pack and a canoe, fishing rods and some tackle, but little food and no bait or artificial lures. We would portage the boat deep into the bush from lake to lake. For food we would rely on the fish we catch and the mushrooms and herbs we pick in the forest. The boy would see that it does not take just any "*mushi*" to catch a fish, and that there exist all kinds of intricate relations between different forms of life in a certain place. He would find that his hard-gained knowledge of one lake does not necessarily apply to another one just five miles away.

Fishing is more than a hobby to Mr. Ibuse. It is a craft and a discipline not unlike writing itself. It is a sobering experience, for what we call objective knowledge in the city must be tested in the unique network of relations that bind the life in a river or lake. Any romantic illusions about "beautiful nature" must withstand the same practical test. As one of his wise old fishermen says: "Listen, if you don't use baby-bees for bait on this river at this time of the year, you're out of business." (*Kotatsubana*)

I know the counterarguments: "We don't need to know which mushroom is edible and which lethal nowadays. We don't have to know which bait gets fish and which does not for our survival. All we need is a knowledge of which buttons to push on the emotional keyboard of our parents or superiors to get what we want, and how to operate the automated machines in our man-made world."

Yet the nostalgia and an increasing need for a world "out there" remains. But compared to popular TV idyls about a non-existent countryside that do not even come close to the distinctive character of the local culture they are supposed to portray, Mr. Ibuse's fishing stories always enable a meeting and a dialogue between two different kinds of experience. His protagonist in a story like *Kotatsubana* is a modern city traveller who has few romantic illusions about the countryside and its people. But he is willing to listen and to look around.

"Listen, Grandpa, how come you get so many fish? Won't you teach me how to hook these brookies? There is some kind of trick to it, isn't there?"

"Don't ask me, just watch the fish. They'll teach you."

Some of the information that the old man of the valley offers may be very practical and in fact help one to get fish; some may be just an amusing angler's yarn. But the overall feeling one gets from this encounter of town and country is one of genuine human communication and mutual respect. What is more, the good-natured way in which the two tease each other rings with Mr. Ibuse's gentle humor.

Yet Ibuse Masuji does not just go fishing to the remote valleys where mountain streams are born. He seems to know a secret path to the very source of the Japanese language. How else could he have discovered unique flowers like *kotatsubana* and *odenbana* that city dwellers have not even heard of?

These names reveal a great deal about the imagination that created them. Only people who feel as much at home in the outdoors as in their houses could have invented these names. These flowers do exist somewhere in the valleys and mountains of Shinshū. But even if they did not, Mr. Ibuse could have created them. Such is his power with words and his insight into the hearts of his people.

When the fisherman of *Kotatsubana* comes back to Tokyo, he opens his encyclopedia and looks for the *kotatsu* and *oden* flowers he saw in the mountains. But all he can find are several "pink family" (*nadeshiko ka*) plants that resemble the real thing. And this is the moral: a world without a *kotatsubana* is a poorer world. The clue to our original humanity which we all share can not be found "back in Tokyo" in the generalities of an encyclopedia. We must look for it somewhere higher up the stream, closer to the springs of our particular imagination and our particular language. The higher we go, the more the languages may differ. But we might be getting closer to an essential human experience that can be shared. After all, genuine communication can only take place between genuine identities. The man who knows *kotatsu* and *oden* flowers has more identity than the one who knows only that there is something like a "pink family."

[Note] IBUSE MASUJI (b. 1898) has had a longer career than almost every major Japanese novelist writing today. He is not yet well known in the West, but perhaps this is because he is deeply rooted in Japanese soil, and it is difficult to translate his appealing way of expression which depends on a subtle choice of words. He is an intellectual writer who keeps his sharp observations of human psychology slightly hidden beneath the surface. His style, beautifully combining rich humor with a touch of pathos, is like mellow wine, gently intoxicating readers' hearts.
1. Dragonfly 2. A variety of dragonfly 3. A white butterfly 4. A yellow butterfly.

ÔOKA SHÔHEI—

The Experience of War in Literature

JEAN ESMEIN

Upon their departure for war, some men turn their backs on life; others enter into it more thoughtfully. Hateful though war may be, it can give sterling human qualities—courage, sincerity—a positive chance to overcome faults such as vanity and falsehood which, even in times of peace, are capable of leading men of good will astray.

In one of his best known speeches before the National Assembly of France, André Malraux said that culture is that which has survived sex and death. Death, like sex, provokes violent excitement which dealers in amusements take part in. Such works are perishable, and culture soon forgets them.

Ôoka Shôhei's books on war are devoted to reviving the experiences of men who lived within the very vicinity of death. He writes of war seen through the eyes of men, and of death divested of its last convulsions. The survivors retain these memories, their gaze tinged with profound sorrow and bountiful forgiveness. Though the events he depicts are ephemeral, they are capable of inspiring men to survive death, and one can be certain that culture will retain them.

Of course there are the official histories, which strip war and its events of all embellishment, of all romantic attributes. But these are uninspiring, characterized by prolixity, giving superfluous information on events of no importance, but the most meager information on those times when men experience intense emotions.

Reconstructing this recent period in history with exactitude, through the eyes of those who have lived it, or through the eyes of their parents, has been for Ôoka Shôhei an affair so serious that he has not been satisfied with consulting the records of armies; he has read the personal documents of the men who fought the battles (letters, notebooks, diaries), all the documents he has been able to lay hands on.

Ôoka has devoted to the war a great part of his literary activity, as though the war were not yet terminated, and as though he were indebted to those who had fought it with him. He did not approve of the war. One can also say that he did not approve of the government that brought about this war. There is, in his character, a blending of two opposites: first, the rebel who disapproves of the system fabricated in the name of the state in order to control the destinies of men; then there is the loyalist that makes him accept the trials endured in common with his countrymen.

Even though the state may be of ambiguous identity, relations with the state during war become personal. Ôoka Shôhei's chronicles and novels of war are devoted to personal relations which have produced nothing but undeserved suffering. The issue of the battles— the defeat—is, moreover, nothing but a sudden change of situation. To judge the war by its results would only mean rewriting the official history.

The experience of war has no equivalent, perhaps because for men engaged in the conflict it is in itself proof of their having transcended death; but those who write of war often tend to a bombastic style. Ôoka Shôhei does not. Hemingway thought that there were two kinds of writers: those who went to war, and those who did not, but will always be aware that it is an experience that they have missed.

Some combatants never expect victory, and so from the very start, they prepare for the final resistance. Others can think of nothing but victory, thus they are ready to throw away their lives in desperate deeds. Others have known war only as a discussion of strategy around a gaming table. The errors of each group lead to unbelievable misfortune, despair, and misery.

One cannot help comparing Ôoka's books with other excellent volumes on contemporary war, like those of Alexander Solzhenitsyn. In *August 1914*, the intent to underline errors is obvious; but, as with Ôoka, the author's portrayal of men surpasses his narration of the events of war.

When, even after an attack, the author still knows nothing of the situation, there is nothing he can do but narrate events to the best of his ability, with no attempt àt organization. Ôoka judges strategies without leniency; he writes like an engineer; he renders an account of where, how, under whose orders, at what time, in what inclemencies of weather, how clad, and eating what, the men survived death.

Fundamentally this is what all writers wish they were capable of doing. Hemingway confirms this; for the history of the man who, at the brink of death, has caught glimpses of the other side of life is one of the supreme themes in literature.

(Tr. by Sister Marie Philomène)

[Note] ÔOKA SHÔHEI (b. 1909) studied French literature when he was a young man and became known as a scholar and translator of Stendahl. When the Second World War began he was drafted into the infantry as a private at the age of thirty-five, and was sent to the Philippines. When the army was routed toward the end of the war he suffered from hunger and exhaustion and was taken prisoner by the American army. These experiences became the kernel for his later fiction. Returning to Japan he wrote *Prisoner of War* and *Fires on the Plain*, and won the high critical praise as a novelist. His self-consciousness, or extremely sharp observation of the human consciousness, together with his lucid style, have become a kind of standard for modern Japanese literature.

Recently he completed a long and detailed account of the fighting between Japanese and Americans on the island of Leyte, entitled *A Chronicle of the Battle of Leyte*. When asked, "Why write about the war now?" he replies, "It is the duty of those who survived."

Mishima Yukio—

On Translating Textures

Meredith Weatherby

Of all modern Japanese authors Mishima Yukio has doubtless been the most frequently translated into English. He has at times been most fortunate in his translators—and at others most unfortunate. Without determining into which category I fall, I should like to talk briefly about my experience in making the first two translations of his works to appear in English—*Kamen no Kokuhaku* (*Confessions of a Mask*) and *Shiosai* (*The Sound of Waves*).

As a matter of fact, I have been complimented upon my translations by British and American readers whose opinions I value. But the Japanese who have read them, often comparing them word by word with the originals, have been much more critical, pointing out how very much my English versions differ from the Japanese. And this observation is quite correct. My aim was never to produce literal translations but to re-form Mishima's thoughts and style in such a way as to create the story I think he himself would have written if he had been writing in English as his native language. I believe strongly that this is the only way to approach the translation of any Japanese literary work: anything short of a complete re-creation is sure to sound unnatural in its English version.

Kamen no Kokuhaku was the first Mishima translation I made, though it was published, by New Directions, some time after my translation of *Shiosai*, which was published by Knopf. I worked on the first translation in my spare time for almost two years. By the time I finished my first draft I had amassed a great many questions that only the author could answer. Fortunately, just at that time Mishima came to America on his first visit and I was able to meet him in New York with my list of questions. Given the great subtlety of Mishima's prose style and his innate love of words and relish in using them delicately in very intricate and convoluted sentences, it was natural that almost all my questions concerned fine shades of meaning. Pointing to a passage in the original, I would ask him whether he meant this or that. Usually he would quickly give me a positive answer. But there were also a number of times when, after reading the passage several times, he would finally shake his head in puzzlement and say: "I wonder what I did mean there." And what was I, the translator, to do with a passage whose meaning was not even clear to the author? Generally I tried to leave such passages equally enigmatic in English, though it is more difficult to be intentionally vague in English than in Japanese.

My visit with Mishima on that occasion lasted through the night, and we finally stumbled out of his hotel, bleary-eyed, into a cold dawn for a cup of coffee before parting, he to return to Japan and I to polish my translation in light of his answers to my questions. It was a memorable experience, one I have treasured through the years.

Probably it was out of pity for my struggles with the subtle difficulties of *Kamen no Kokuhaku* that Mishima suggested I next translate *Shiosai*. As he himself recognized, this was intentionally a much simpler piece of writing, and its translation went much more smoothly, so much so that I fear I became over-confident and fell into such traps of mistranslation as speaking of Kyoto's Shimizu Temple instead of Kiyomizu Temple—a mistake that Mishima and I were to laugh over in later years.

Unfortunately, I became so occupied with my own affairs that I never again had the pleasure of translating Mishima: the task of translating literature from Japanese to English is so formidable that one can never hope for adequate financial benefits but must find recompense in the pleasure of the act alone. Certainly I enjoyed translating Mishima tremendously and feel I have a better understanding of those two novels of his than of any other novels I have ever read. I handled, as it were, each and every word in the novels, feeling their textures and coming to understand the tremendous artistry with which they were woven into sentences of great beauty, paragraphs of magic, chapters of deep emotions, novels of enduring worth. For all of this, as for his friendship, I shall always be most thankful to Mishima the writer and Mishima the man.

[Note]   MISHIMA YUKIO (1925-1970) was endowed with literary genius from the time he was quite young, publishing his first collection of short stories, *A Forest in Flower*, at the age of nineteen. His reputation as a novelist became established after the Second World War with the success of his semi-autobiographical novel *Confessions of a Mask*, followed by *Forbidden Colors, The Sound of Waves, The Temple of the Golden Pavilion*, and others. He also demonstrated exceptional talent as a playwright, among his successes being *Modern Noh Plays, Madame de Sade*, and *Our Friend Hitler*. Of all Japanese writers, he is one of the most translated and best known outside of Japan.

In his later years he became the spokesman for an esthetic sort of nationalism. As soon as he had completed his last major work, a tetralogy entitled *The Sea of Fertility*, he entered the Self Defense Forces Headquarters, made a speech urging a coup d'etat, and then committed ritual suicide by disembowelment, causing a sensation throughout the world.

ABE KÔBÔ—

The "International Style" in Japanese Literature

ANDREW HORVAT

Despite the immense popularity of *Woman in the Dunes*, *Face of Another*, and *The Ruined Map*, Abe Kôbô has no public image in his own country. This is all the stranger because in Japan authors are always in the limelight, their opinions sought by newspapers, their autographs by eager fans. But other than the occasional interviews he grants to journalists, usually after some prodding from his publishers, Abe does nothing to cultivate a personal following.

Abe also dislikes being called an "international writer," that is, someone foreigners can understand. Such mild praise from some critics often means that the person referred to as "international" lacks "purely" Japanese characteristics, which foreigners are not supposed to be able to fathom.

Abe's popularity abroad is not due to any exotic appeal. His novels are devoid of cherry blossoms or plum trees in bloom. If anything, it is the lack of such decorative japonoiserie that allows readers far away to relate to Abe's heroes in a very direct way.

"The heroes of my novels are inhabitants of modern cities," says Abe.

I remember an expression from *The Deaf Girl*, one of his early short stories. "Her apartment faced on a mislaid streetcorner." That sentence is the only clue the reader has of where the scene is set. There is no suggestion of any particular country.

One of the factors contributing to Abe's popularity among readers living in industrialized nations is the author's positive attitude toward having no roots, i.e. being in limbo but enjoying it. In a way this attitude is similar to that of the British psychologist R.D. Laing, who claims neurosis is not a disease. Rather it is a sign of intelligence being used. In the same way, Abe hesitates to call rootlessness alienation.

In his essay *Uchinaru Henkyô*, Abe describes the dangers of what can happen when people are constantly forced to relate to their roots, as in Nazi Germany. The Nazi persecution of urbanized Jewry was a corollary of the Nazi's elevation of German peasant virtues. The peasants were tied to the soil. The Jews were not.

Abe's distrust of any ideology which places birthplace or home village at its pinnacle is complete. The last short autobiographical note he wrote in 1966 is proof positive of this:

I was born in Tokyo and brought up in Manchuria. The place of family origin on my papers, however, is in Hokkaidô, and I have lived there for a few years. In short, my place of birth, the place where I was brought up, and my place of family origin, are three different points on the map. Thanks to this fact, it is a difficult matter for me to write even an abbreviated list of important dates in my life. Essentially, I am a man without a hometown. That much I can say. And the feeling of hometown-phobia which flows at the base of my emotions, may be attributable to my background. I am put off by anything which is valued only because it is stationary.

I shall never forget the experience of interpreting for Abe when he was talking to a young American director who wanted to film one of Abe's novels in Japan. Abe told the young man to try making the film in England, or the U.S., or in fact any country where he could get quick credit and good actors.

The young man was visibly perplexed. He could not imagine the setting as being anywhere other than the country where the novel was set. Abe finally convinced the young director that the novel is about the sea and the land and about people having to change all of a sudden in order to adapt to a new environment, and it makes little difference whether the setting is Tokyo, London or San Francisco.

It would be rather difficult to imagine the late Kawabata Yasunari arguing that the tea ceremony in *Thousand Cranes* be set in Darjeeling or that all those color cinemascope versions of the *Snow Country* could be done more cheaply in Spain because a mountain is a mountain is a mountain is a mountain.

But Abe's being a controversial writer has to do with his trying to talk about universal dilemmas of men living in industrial societies, in a country where many people are still, even after a hundred years of industrialization, convinced of their inalienable uniqueness.

It is already commonplace to say that Japan's industrialization was achieved by traditional social patterns of loyalty and paternalism. Neither is it unusual for social critics to report that the very fruits of industrialization, the privacy afforded by the automobile, the house, the nuclear family, the mobility offered by university education, that all of these things are conspiring to destroy the social fabric which enabled progress to occur in the first place.

In response to their alienation many Japanese are turning to symbols of old Japan in order to reassure themselves of their cultural identities. Perhaps it is for such reasons that Mishima Yukio and Kawabata Yasunari have become the objects of veneration. Their expressions of sadness at the passing of older virtues offer a comforting aura of tradition in an age when Japanese businessmen in New York or London jostle in subways not much different from those in Tokyo.

But Abe's novels offer none of the comforts of home.

[Note] ABE KÔBÔ (b. 1924) is perhaps better known to foreign readers than any other contemporary Japanese writer, thanks to numerous translations. He began his literary activity after the Second World War, expressing an existentialist viewpoint, and was involved with communism for a while. The themes he treats are problems of human alienation in a capitalistic society, and his style is full of hidden meanings and satire. His themes are realities that can be discovered on any streetcorner throughout the contemporary world, and this is one reason why he has gained an international reputation.

Abe is considered to be the standard bearer of *avant-garde* literature in Japan. He is also well known as a playwright, and has become even more popular through film versions of his novels, such as *Woman in the Dunes*.

Endô Shûsaku —

Depicting the Foreigner as a Human Being

Paul C. Blum

In Japanese literature, the foreigner, the Westerner, has not fared badly. Yet, if he appears at all in a novel or short story it is little more than as a shadowy figure, a mere suggestion of a character. Never has a full-length portrait been attempted. Today, this is no longer true. *Chinmoku* (*Silence*), by Endô Shûsaku, is the notable exception. In this historical novel, for the first time in Japanese literature we not only have a foreigner, a priest, assuming the principal role, but he is presented in human dimensions.

Father Sebastian Rodrigues, the protagonist, was one of that brave band of Catholic missionaries who, in the seventeenth century, despite the proscription and the religious persecutions, ventured to enter Japan secretly to bring solace and support to the Christian converts living in hiding, and also to try to find Father Ferreira, his former teacher, whose reported apostasy had scandalized the Church. The book tells of Rodrigues' capture, his suffering, and his apostasy.

It is a profoundly moving story. Although the priest is spared the physical tortures that he is made to witness, his participation in the agony of the converts, the anguish he feels as his own faith wavers, are so real, so humanly portrayed, that certain pages are painful to read. Nowhere, at any time, are we reminded that the author is Japanese, that the torture of body and soul endured by this Portuguese priest is being probed by a Japanese. Mr. Endô is a Catholic and, therefore, certainly sensitive to Rodrigues' dilemma, but in describing the spiritual torment, in explaining the apostasy, he has chosen the Western rather than the Japanese interpretation. During the interrogation by the infamous Governor Inouye of Nagasaki, the Father is warned that he will be inevitably defeated by the "swamp of Japan," the intolerant soil of Japan that deforms, when it does not wither, all beliefs and ideals that are not native to it. And this is confirmed by Ferreira whom Rodrigues finally meets in his darkest hour. In a dramatic confrontation, Ferreira admits that he as well as others were conquered by "the swamp that is Japan." Endô rejects this explanation. It is the silence of God that defeated Rodrigues, he intimates; in those lonely hours in prison, filled with physical misery, listening to the cries of the tortured Christians and waiting for a similar doom, it is the silence that defeats the priest, the unbearable lack of response to his anguish and his prayers.

Father Rodrigues is an historical figure, appearing here under an assumed name. Little is known regarding his arrival in Japan, his capture, imprisonment, and subsequent apostasy. Using the few recorded facts, Mr. Endô has woven the story skillfully. Whether the details are fact or fiction is of little consequence: the foreign priest is alive and suffers in these pages; and from them emerges to take his place in Japanese literature.

The book ends with a brief and bald account, taken from official Edo records, of the surveillance and activities of the household of one Okada San'yemon, once known as Father Sebastian Rodrigues. His death, at the age of 64, is reported. The story of those last thirty tortured years is left untold.

[Note] ENDÔ SHÛSAKU (b. 1923) is a Catholic writer who studied in France during the 1950's. Returning to Japan, he first attracted attention with his novel *White Men*, and established his reputation with *The Sea and Poison*, based on an actual vivisection case during the war. Endô's works frequently deal with the religious sense of the Japanese, or their consciousness of sin as seen from a Catholic's point of view.

An Intellectual Curiosity About Women

DAVID THARP

It is often said that Japan consists of two distinct sides—the *"ura"*,[1] the gloomy, dark, brooding, heavily introspective side of Japan's character, and the *"omote"*,[2] the sophisticated social face which is composed of many intellectual subtleties.

It is in the latter that Yoshiyuki Junnosuke excels as a short story writer. He deals masterfully with the social complexities of Japanese psychology and behavior. In his intellectual approach he is an unemotional, uninvolved observer who writes of a situation without altering the fabric of the surroundings around his characters.

Yoshiyuki writes of people in their microcosmic worlds without any artificial cosmetic posturing that would otherwise detract from the naturalness of the story. There are no long, complicated plots; rather he concentrates on intense, short spans of time which reveal people as they are.

One comment that Yoshiyuki often makes in regard to his stories is that he takes a "cell" from life and then tries to infer from seemingly unrelated cells an organic whole.

It is interesting that many of Yoshiyuki's stories center around the lives of prostitutes. His interest is not sensual like Nagai Kafû. He relegates the sensual to second place while making penetrating intellectual observations through the eyes of characters who seem to have completely disinterested involvements.

His most famous story about this theme is *Shôfu no Heya* (*The Prostitute's Room*). In this story a young man looking for psychological security meets a sympathetic prostitute by the name of Akiko with whom he is able to create a continuous, intimate relationship without becoming emotionally or romantically involved.

Despite the physical liaison between the young man and the girl,

Yoshiyuki calculatedly maintains a careful distance between the two, giving one the impression that the young man's interest in the girl is like a person calmly appreciating a portrait in an art gallery.

In this sense there is a sharp difference between Yoshiyuki's presentation of the "I" novel and the confessional nature of other "I" novelists. Although one looks at life through the lives of Yoshiyuki's characters from the perspective of the first person, there is still an insistence by the writer upon the prerogatives of third person objectivity. Eventually the young man and the prostitute drift apart, and both seem fatalistically acceptant that this is the way that it was meant to be from the beginning. In this story one can see clearly Yoshiyuki's "cellular" concept coming into play. Having experienced Akiko's world, or her "cell" as represented by her room, the young man draws an abstract understanding of the rest of her life—the organic whole.

One may ask the question how Yoshiyuki can maintain such a detachment between his characters without having them crossing any emotional barriers to deeper involvement.

It seems that Yoshiyuki takes some joy in his cool intellectual control of himself and the people in his stories. The compartmentalization of life can give a freedom to the main actor whose enjoyment comes from being able to draw all the experiences in the separate "cells" together into a single, mutual relationship.

Yoshiyuki's intellectual curiosity subjects the highly emotional potential of sex, anxiety, decadence, and sensual passion to a sharp, sensitive discipline. He is intimate without the responsibility of commitment compromising his involvements, and if there is any possibility of shame arising from an action, he takes great pains to cover the emotions with a sophisticated cloak of rationality.

Raw feelings are suppressed and controlled at the intellectual level by the characters in Yoshiyuki's stories. He shows how non-committal many people actually are to each other despite involvements at other levels of feeling.

Yoshiyuki is a good example of those intellectuals who have been socialized in the Pacific coast side of Japan. One must be quick to make decisions about determining the roles to be played in certain social situations of Japanese urban culture, for without this complex sense of interpreting situations one would soon be at a loss with one's peers.

For centuries the currents of history and culture have crossed along the lines of communication between Tokyo and the cities to the south along the Pacific coast. It was required that one be a good observer and sensitive to the demands of those around you. From this sensitivity a highly complicated, non-verbal appreciation and understanding for the psychology of the other person emerged as second nature to many socialized Japanese.

Yoshiyuki stands out as a keen observer of the Japanese in this regard. It is perhaps because of this that he gained so much popularity among many people who probably recognize their own inner personalities through his penetrating portrayals of life.

[Note] YOSHIYUKI JUNNOSUKE was born in Okayama in 1924, attended Shizuoka High School and later entered the English Department at Tokyo University. He is one of the novelists who appeared following the first wave of postwar writers. The first group frequently dealt with ideological themes, but later writers like Yoshiyuki took for their themes the subtle psychological nuances of everyday life. Treating these subjects with a blend of detached humor and pathos, Yoshiyuki and his contemporaries have come to occupy an important place in Japan's literary world. This change in literary approach corresponds to the change in Japanese society from the confusion of the postwar period to the revival of a strong middle class.

Yoshiyuki is known for his treatment of the world of prostitutes and the relations between the sexes. Sex is always an important theme in his novels, but it is always examined with a cool and clinical eye.

1. Behind the superficial face of things. 2. The façade.

KAIKÔ TAKESHI —

The Long Way Home

MIKOLAJ MELANOWICZ

Kaikô Takeshi is an author who has much to say, but of matters not easy to speak of; so that in treating them he often rejects established conventions of plot and conventional forms of literary expression. Several journeys around the world have given him the chance not only to witness the trial of Eichmann, the wars in Vietnam, Biafra and in the Middle East, but also to observe those Japanese who have been unable to find a place in their own country and thus roam about the world learning the bitterness of isolation. All of these experiences are at the roots of the world depicted in the novel *Darkness in Summer* (*Natsu no Yami*, 1972), a sequel to an earlier novel *Bright Darkness* (*Kagayakeru Yami*, 1968). *Darkness in Summer* continues the theme of slackness and sensual satiation of man in "a time of soft bellies," and ultimately demands a rejection of inert sensual vegetation for positive action.

The novel takes place somewhere in Europe. The author does not name towns or countries, except Vietnam. The narrator, the main character of the novel, is on a journey. He drinks, eats and sleeps, leading a life void of any action. One day he meets a former girl friend, a Japanese who now lives in Europe. Love is introduced to their daily routine.

After a week they both move to a country in which the woman has lived and studied for years, probably West Germany, and the town of their stay is Bonn. The man suffers from feelings of hopelessness and melancholy which overwhelm him "like dirty water." He recalls events from his last stay in Saigon, and notes that his past ten years have been spent on journeys. After a time they go to the lakeside in the mountains. Here they experience simple human joy, and gain strength and faith in life. Their return to the town, however, brings back feelings of boredom and laziness. The woman reads to her friend a fragment from a newspaper about the military actions in Vietnam. It moves him and he decides to leave, although his friend begs him to stay with her. "You simply want to run away . . .," she says. "You refuse just to decay, and so you spin round like a top. You can only stand when you're turning round . . . Nobody is asking you to go there and die like a dog by a bucket of rubbish. Is this your great dream?"

Darkness in Summer is an exquisitely written novel; its action is uniform and its rhythm consistent. The author is examining the wounds of his own generation, which in spite of everything has not stopped yearning for natural and simple sensitivity. Life which consists in satisfying the senses is deceptive. The only escape from this kind of "darkness" that the author seems to see is action.

The author's acute observations on human nature, presented through these two Japanese detached from their own culture, raise questions about life that make the novel interesting to Japanese, European, and American readers alike.

There is, however, a certain ideological weakness in the novel which lies in his somewhat vague definition of the value of "action." We know that the man decides to go back to Vietnam, to which he is attracted by memories. But for what purpose does he go there? Is it to observe things happening in a foreign country? Or to fight? And if so, then on which side? He is, after all, a Japanese who outside of Japan will feel excluded from the "local" rhythm of life, or will be considered a stranger. This is well illustrated in *Bright Darkness*. He does not, however, return to his country. Why not?

Bright Darkness in Vietnam and *Darkness in Summer* in Europe present the man at bay, caught in a tight circle of his internal struggles. He has no prospect of winning this battle—this he knows well. However, he still believes that by leaving for distant parts of the world he will find some relationship between the world's and his own problems. This undeclared trust is a source of strength for this man adrift, this man who on the verge of exhaustion sees a spark of hope glowing somewhere far away.

One would hope that the hero will come back to Japan in one of Kaikô's subsequent novels. This ambitious and courageous writer is left with no other choice. Through Vietnam and Europe he will eventually reach his own country; the most difficult of all to write about. For its inhabitants now know all the faces of the contemporary world and this has made their own lives no easier. As the maxim says: more knowledge means more suffering. After reading Kaikô's novels I am convinced that the author's own life illustrates the truth of this saying.

[Note] KAIKÔ TAKESHI (b. 1930) and Ôye Kenzaburô are the youngest of Japan's established novelists. They are no longer really "young," but no writers after them have gained a comparable critical evaluation. Kaikô was born in Osaka and is endowed with the energetic, tenacious disposition typical of Osaka merchants. He is a man of action with many interests, which have ranged from covering the war in Vietnam as a writer to fishing in rivers and lakes all over the world. His most recent novels, *Bright Darkness* and *Darkness in Summer*, are perhaps his best works. He is one of the novelists from whom we can expect outstanding work in the future.

Bibliography

and

Chronological Table

BIBLIOGRAPHY: JAPAN'S LITERATURE IN ENGLISH TRANSLATIONS

(Translations Related to the 40 Essays)

Classics:

Kojiki 古 事 記
KOJIKI Tr. by Shunji Inouye. Fukuoka, Nihon Shuji Kyôiku Renmei, 1966.
KOJIKI Tr. by Donald L. Philippi. Tokyo, Univ. of Tokyo Press, 1968.
TRANSLATION OF 'KO-JI-KI' or RECORDS OF ANCIENT MATTERS Tr. by Basil Hall Chamberlain. Kobe, J. L. Thompson & Co. Ltd., 1932.

Mannyôshû 万 葉 集
THE MANYOSHU Tr. by H. H. Honda. Tokyo, Hokuseidô, 1967.
THE MANYOSHU Tr. by Donald Keene. N. Y., Columbia Univ. Press, 1965.

Taketori Monogatari 竹 取 物 語
THE OLD BAMBOO-HEWER'S STORY or THE TALE OF TAKETORI Tr. by Frederick Victor Dickens. Tokyo, San Kaku Sha, 1934.

Makura no Sôshi 枕 草 子
THE PILLOW BOOK OF SEI SHÔNAGON Tr. by Ivan Morris. N.Y., Columbia Univ. Press, 1967.

Genji Monogatari 源 氏 物 語
THE TALE OF GENJI Tr. by Arthur Waley. N.Y., Modern Library, 1960.

Konjaku Monogatari 今 昔 物 語
AGES AGO Tr. by S.W. Jones. Cambridge, Harvard Univ. Press, 1959.

Heike Monogatari 平 家 物 語
THE TALE OF THE HEIKE Tr. by Hiroshi Kitagawa. Introduction by Edward Seidensticker. Tokyo, Univ. of Tokyo Press, 1974.
THE TEN-FOOT SQUARE HUT AND TALES OF THE HEIKE Tr. by A.L. Sadler. Tokyo, Tuttle, 1972.

Tannishô 歎 異 抄
TANNISHO Kyoto, Higashi Honganji, 1961.
THE TANNISHO Tr. by Ryôsetsu Fujiwara. Kyoto, Ryûkoku Univ., 1962.

Tsurezuregusa 徒 然 草
ESSAYS IN IDLENESS Tr. by Donald Keene. N.Y., Columbia Univ. Press, 1967.

ZE'AMI 世 阿 弥 (1362?–1443)
KADENSHO Tr. by Chûichi Sakurai and others. Kyoto, Sumiya Shinobe Publishing Institute, 1968.

Tauye Zôshi 田 植 草 紙
THE GENIAL SEED Tr. by Frank Hoff. Tokyo, Mushinsha, 1971.

IHARA SAIKAKU 井 原 西 鶴 (1642–1693)
FIVE WOMEN WHO LOVED LOVE Tr. by Wm.

Theodore de Bary. Tokyo, Tuttle, 1956.
THE JAPANESE FAMILY STOREHOUSE or THE MILLIONAIRES' GOSPEL MODERNIZED Tr. by G.W. Sargent. Cambridge, Univ. Press, 1959.
THE LIFE OF AN AMOROUS MAN Tr. by Kengi Hamada. Rutland, Vt., Tuttle, 1964.
THE LIFE OF AN AMOROUS WOMAN, AND OTHER WRITINGS Ed. and tr. by Ivan Morris. N.Y., New Directions, 1963.
THIS SCHEMING WORLD Tr. by Masamori Takatsuka and David C. Stubbs. Rutland, Vt., Tuttle, 1965.

MATSUO BASHÔ 松 尾 芭 蕉 (1644–1694)
ANTHOLOGY OF JAPANESE LITERATURE *Prose Poem on the Unreal Dwelling. The Narrow Road of Oku.* Tr. by Donald Keene; *Haiku by Bashô and His School.* Tr. by Harold G. Henderson.
BACK ROADS TO FAR TOWNS Tr. by Cid Corman and Susumu Kamaike. Tokyo, Mushinsha, 1968.
ASIA MAJOR Bashô's Journey of 1864. Tr. by Donald Keene. 7, pts. 1-2, Dec. 1959.
TRANSACTIONS OF THE ASIATIC SOCIETY OF JAPAN Bashô's Journey to Sarashina. Tr. by Donald Keene. 3rd. series. v5.
THE NARROW ROAD TO THE DEEP NORTH, AND OTHER TRAVEL SKETCHES Tr. by Nobuyuki Yuasa. Harmondsworth, Penguin Books, 1966.

CHIKAMATSU MONZAYEMON 近松門左衛門 (1653–1724)
MAJOR PLAYS OF CHIKAMATSU Tr. by Donald Keene. N.Y., Columbia Univ. Press, 1961.

YOSA BUSON 与 謝 蕪 村 (1716–1783)
A HISTORY OF HAIKU Tr. by R.H. Blyth. Tokyo, Hokuseidô Press, 1963.
AN ANTHOLOGY OF HAIKU, ANCIENT AND MODERN Tr. by Asatarô Miyamori. Tokyo, Taiseidô Press, 1967.

UYEDA AKINARI 上 田 秋 成 (1734–1809)
TALES OF MOONLIGHT AND RAIN Tr. by Kengi Hamada. Tokyo, Univ. of Tokyo Press, 1971.

Modern:

ABE KÔBÔ 安 部 公 房 (b. 1924)
FOUR STORIES BY KOBO ABE Tr. by Andrew Horvat. Tokyo, Hara Shobô, 1973.
FRIENDS Tr. by Donald Keene. N.Y., Grove Press, 1969; Tokyo, Tuttle, 1970.
INTER ICE AGE 4 Tr. by E. Dale Saunders. N.Y., Knopf, 1970; Tokyo, Tuttle, 1970; London, Cape, 1971.
THE FACE OF ANOTHER Tr. by E. Dale Saunders. N.Y., Knopf, 1966; Tokyo, Tuttle, 1967; London, Weidenfeld and Nicolson, 1969.
THE RUINED MAP Tr. by E. Dale Saunders. N.Y.,

Knopf, 1969; Tokyo, Tuttle, 1970.
THE WOMAN IN THE DUNES Tr. by E. Dale
Saunders. N.Y., Knopf, 1964; Tokyo, Tuttle, 1965;
London, Secker and Warburg, 1965.

AKUTAGAWA RYÛNOSUKE　芥川龍之介
(1892–1927)
A FOOL'S LIFE Tr. by Will Petersen. Tokyo,
Mushinsha, 1970.
EXOTIC JAPANESE STORIES *The Kappa* and other
15 stories. Tr. by Takashi Kojima and John McVittie.
N.Y., Liveright, 1964.
HELL SCREEN AND OTHER STORIES Tr. by W. H.
H. Norman. Tokyo, Hokuseidô, 1948; N. Y., Green-
wood, 1971.
JAPANESE SHORT STORIES *The Nose* and other 9
stories. Tr. by Takashi Kojima. N. Y., Liveright, 1961;
N. Y., Avon Books, 1963.
KAPPA Tr. by Seiichi Shiojiri. Osaka, Akitaya, 1947;
Tokyo, Hokuseidô, 1949.
KAPPA Tr. by Geoffrey Bownas. London, Peter
Owen, 1970; Tokyo, Tuttle, 1970.
MODERN JAPANESE LITERATURE *Hell Screen* and
other story. Tr. by W. H. H. Norman. Ed. by Donald
Keene. N. Y., Grove, 1956; Tokyo, Tuttle, 1957.
MODERN JAPANESE STORIES *The Painting of an
Autumn Mountain*. Ed. and tr. by Ivan Morris.
London, Eyre and Spottiswoode, 1961; Tokyo, Tuttle,
1962.
POSTHUMOUS WORKS OF RYUNOSUKE AKUTA-
GAWA *Life of a Certain Fool* and other story. Tr. by
Akio Inouye. Tenri, Tenri Jihôsha, 1961.
RASHOMON AND OTHER STORIES Tr. by Takashi
Kojima. N. Y., Liveright, 1952; Tokyo, Tuttle, 1952.
RASHOMON AND OTHER STORIES Tr. by Glenn
W. Shaw. Tokyo, Hara Shobô, 1964
TALES GROTESQUE AND CURIOUS *Rashomon* and
other 10 stories. Tr. by Glenn W. Shaw. Tokyo, Hoku-
seidô, 1930.
THE THREE TREASURES AND OTHER STORIES
FOR CHILDREN *The Spider's Thread* and other 5
stories. Tr. by Takamasa Sasaki. Tokyo, Hokuseidô,
1944.

DAZAI OSAMU　太宰　　治　　(1909–1948)
MODERN JAPANESE LITERATURE *Villon's Wife*.
Ed. and tr. by Donald Keene. N. Y., Grove Press,
1956; Tokyo, Tuttle, 1957.
MODERN JAPANESE SHORT STORIES *O-san*. Tr. by
E. G. Seidensticker. Tokyo, Japan Pub. Trading Co.,
1960.
MODERN JAPANESE STORIES *The Courtesy Call*.
Ed. and tr. by Ivan Morris. London, Eyre and Spot-
tiswoode, 1961; Tokyo, Tuttle, 1962.
NO LONGER HUMAN Tr. by Donald Keene. N. Y.,
New Directions, 1958; London, Owen, 1957; London,
Four Square Press, 1961.
THE DECLINING SUN Tr. by Takehide Kikuchi.
Tokyo, Nire Shobô, 1950.
THE JAPANESE IMAGE *The Visitor*. Tr. by Ivan
Morris. Ed. by M. Schneps and A. D. Coox. Tokyo,
Orient West, 1965.
THE JAPANESE IMAGE *A Lie*. Tr. by Toshihiko

Satô. Ed. by M. Schneps and A. D. Coox. Tokyo,
Orient West, 1966.
THE SETTING SUN Tr. by Donald Keene. N. Y.,
New Directions, 1956; London, Owen, 1958; London,
Four Square Press, 1961; Tokyo, Hara Shobô, 1965.

ENDÔ SHÛSAKU　遠藤　周作　　(b. 1923)
SEA AND POISON Tr. by Michael Gallagher. London,
Peter Owen, 1971; Tokyo, Tuttle, 1972.
SILENCE Tr. by William Johnston. Tokyo, Sophia
Univ., 1969; Tokyo, Tuttle, 1969; London, Prentice-
Hall, 1970.
THE GOLDEN COUNTRY Tr. by Francis Mathy.
Tokyo, Tuttle, 1970.
WONDERFUL FOOL Tr. by Francis Mathy. London,
Peter Owen, 1974.

HIGUCHI ICHIYÔ　樋口　一葉　　(1872–1896)
MODERN JAPANESE LITERATURE *Growing Up*.
Tr. by Edward Seidensticker. Ed. by Donald Keene. N.
Y., Grove Press, 1956; Tokyo, Tuttle, 1957.
MONUMENTA NIPPONICA Muddy Bay. Tr. by
Hisako Tanaka. v. 14, no. 1-2, 1958.
MONUMENTA NIPPONICA The Thirteenth Night. Tr.
by Hisako Tanaka. v. 14, no. 3-4, 1960-61.
TAKEKURABE *Teenagers Vying for Tops. In the Gut-
ter*. Tr. by Seizô Nobunaga. Tokyo, Information Pub.,
1960.

IBUSE MASUJI　井伏　鱒二　　(b. 1898)
BLACK RAIN Tr. by John Bester. Tokyo, Kôdansha,
1969; London, Secker and Warburg, 1971.
JOHN MANJIRO: THE CAST-AWAY, HIS LIFE AND
ADVENTURES Tr. by Hisakazu Kaneko. Tokyo,
Hokuseidô, 1940.
LIEUTENANT LOOKEAST AND OTHER STORIES
Tr. by John Bester. Tokyo, Kôdansha, 1971.
MODERN JAPANESE STORIES *The Charcoal Bus*.
Ed. and tr. by Ivan Morris. London, Spottiswoode,
1961; Tokyo, Tuttle, 1962.

ISHIKAWA TAKUBOKU　石川　啄木　(1886–1912)
A HANDFUL OF SAND Tr. by Shio Sakanishi.
Boston, Marshall Jones, 1934, 1952.
A SAD TOY Tr. by Hiroshi Takamine. Tokyo, Tokyo
News Service, 1962.
LACQUER BOX *3 Tanka*. Tr. by Kenneth Yasuda.
Tokyo, 1952.
MASTERPIECES OF JAPANESE POETRY ANCIENT
AND MODERN *13 Tanka*. Tr. by Asatarô Miyamori.
Tokyo, Taiseidô, 1956.
MODERN JAPANESE LITERATURE *Wake not. A
Fist. Eleven Waka Poems*. Tr. by Shio Sakanishi. Ed.
by D. Keene N. Y., Grove Press, 1956; Tokyo, Tuttle,
1967.
MODERN JAPANESE POETRY *1 Tanka*. Tr. by
Donald Keene. Ann Arbor, Mich., Center for Japanese
Studies, 1964.
TAKUBOKU: POEMS TO EAT *Handful of Sand. Sad
Toy. Other Poems*. Tr. by Carl Sesar. Tokyo, Kôdan-
sha, 1966; London, Ward Lock, 1966.
THE PENGUIN BOOK OF JAPANESE VERSE *13
Tanka. After a Fruitless Argument. Rather Than Cry*.

Tr. by Geoffrey Bownas and Anthony Thwaite. Harmondsworth, Penguin Books, 1964.
THE POETRY OF ISHIKAWA TAKUBOKU Tr. by H. H. Honda. Tokyo, Hokuseidô, 1959.

KAIKÔ TAKESHI　開高　健　(b. 1930)
DARKNESS IN SUMMER Tr. by Cecilia Segawa Seigle. N. Y., Knopf, 1974.

KAWABATA YASUNARI 川端　康成 (1899–1972)
HOUSE OF THE SLEEPING BEAUTIES AND OTHER STORIES Tr. by Edward Seidensticker. Tokyo, Kôdansha, 1969; London, Quadriga Press, 1969; London, Shere, 1971; N. Y., Ballantine Books, 1970.
JAPAN THE BEAUTIFUL AND MYSELF Tr. by E. G. Seidensticker. Tokyo, Kôdansha, 1969.
MODERN JAPANESE LITERATURE The Mole. Tr. by Edward Seidensticker. Ed. by D. Keene. N. Y., Grove Press, 1956; Tokyo, Tuttle, 1957.
MODERN JAPANESE SHORT STORIES The Mole. Tr. by Edward Seidensticker. Tokyo, Japan Pub. Trad. Co., 1960.
MODERN JAPANESE STORIES The Moon on the Water. Tr. by George Saito. Ed. by I. Morris. London, Spottiswoode, 1961; Tokyo, Tuttle, 1962.
SNOW COUNTRY AND THOUSAND CRANES Tr. by E. G. Seidensticker. N. Y., Knopf, 1969.
THE EXISTENCE AND DISCOVERY OF BEAUTY Tr. by V. H. Viglielmo. Tokyo, Mainichi Shinbunsha, 1969.
THE IZU DANCER Reencounter. Tr. by Leon Picon; The Moon on the Water. Tr. by George Saito; The Mole. The Izu Dancer. Tr. by E. Seidensticker. Tokyo, Hara Shobô, 1963.
THE LAKE Tr. by Reiko Tsukimura. Tokyo, Kôdansha, 1974.
THE SNOW COUNTRY Tr. by Edward Seidensticker. N. Y., Knopf, 1956; London, Secker and Warburg, 1957; Tokyo, Tuttle, 1957.
THE SOUND OF THE MOUNTAIN Tr. by Edward Seidensticker. N. Y., Knopf, 1970; London, Peter Owen, 1970; Tokyo, Tuttle, 1970; London, Secker and Warburg, 1971.
THOUSAND CRANES Tr. by Edward Seidensticker. N. Y., Knopf, 1958; London, Secker and Warburg, 1959; Tokyo, Tuttle, 1960; N. Y., Barkley Pub., 1958.

MASAOKA SHIKI　正岡　子規　(1867–1902)
ANTHOLOGY OF HAIKU ANCIENT AND MODERN 71 Haiku. Tr. by Asatarô Miyamori. Tokyo, Maruzen, 1932.
JAPANESE LITERATURE NEW AND OLD Fruits. Tr. by Ryôzô Matsumoto. Tokyo, Hokuseidô, 1961.
JAPANESE POETIC DIARIES The Verse Record of My Peonies. Tr. by Earl Miner. Berkeley, Univ. of Calif. Press, 1969.
MASTERPIECES OF JAPANESE POETRY ANCIENT AND MODERN The Dews on Pine Leaves. The Milky Way. The Evening-Glories. Tr. by Asatarô Miyamori. Tokyo, Taiseidô, 1936, 1956; N. Y., Greenwood, 1971.
MODERN JAPANESE LITERATURE Eight Haiku

Poems. Tr. by H. G. Henderson. Ed. by D. Keene. N. Y., Grove Press, 1956; Tokyo, Tuttle, 1957.
THE PENGUIN BOOK OF JAPANESE VERSE 2 Tanka and 10 Haiku. Tr. by Geoffrey Bownas and Anthony Thwaite. Harmondsworth, Penguin Books, 1964.
THE WRITING OF IDIOMATIC ENGLISH The Butterflies. Tr. by S. G. Brickley. Tokyo, Kenkyûsha, 1951.

MISHIMA YUKIO　三島由紀夫　(1925–1970)
AFTER THE BANQUET Tr. by Donald Keene. N. Y., Knopf, 1963; Tokyo, Tuttle, 1963; London, Secker and Warburg, 1963.
CONFESSIONS OF A MASK Tr. by Meredith Weatherby, N. Y., New Directions, 1958; London, Peter Owen, 1964; Tokyo, Tuttle, 1970.
DEATH IN MIDSUMMER AND OTHER STORIES Death in Midsummer. Tr. by E. G. Seidensticker, and other 9 stories. N. Y., New Directions, 1966; London, Secker and Warburg, 1967; Harmondsworth, Penguin Books, 1971.
FIVE MODERN NOH PLAYS Tr. by Donald Keene. N. Y., Knopf, 1956; Tokyo, Tuttle, 1967.
FORBIDDEN COLORS Tr. by Alfred H. Marks. N. Y., Knopf, 1968; London, Secker and Warburg, 1968; Tokyo, Tuttle, 1969; Harmondsworth, Penguin Book, 1971.
MADAME DE SADE Tr. by Donald Keene. N. Y., Grove Press, 1967; London, Peter Owen, 1968; Tokyo, Tuttle, 1971.
MODERN JAPANESE SHORT STORIES Death in Midsummer. Tr. by Edward G. Seidensticker. Tokyo, Japan Pub. Trading Co., 1960.
MODERN JAPANESE STORIES The Priest and His Love. Ed. and tr. by Ivan Morris. London, Spottiswoode, 1961; Tokyo, Tuttle, 1962.
RUNAWAY HORSES (The Sea of Fertility v.2) Tr. by Michael Gallagher. N. Y., Knopf, 1973.
SPRING SNOW (The Sea of Fertility v.1) Tr. by Michael Gallagher. N. Y., Knopf, 1971.
SUN AND STEEL Tr. by John Bester. Tokyo, Kôdansha, 1970; London, Secker and Warburg, 1971.
THE DECAY OF THE ANGEL (The Sea of Fertility v.4) Tr. by Edward Seidensticker. N. Y., Knopf, 1974.
THE MENTOR BOOK OF MODERN ASIAN LITERATURE The Temple of the Golden Pavilion. Tr. by Ivan Morris. Ed. by D. B. Shimer. N. Y., New American Library, 1969.
THE SAILOR WHO FELL FROM GRACE WITH THE SEA Tr. by John Nathan. N. Y., Knopf, 1965; London, Secker and Warburg, 1966; Tokyo, Tuttle, 1967; Harmondsworth, Penguin Books, 1970.
THE SOUND OF WAVES Tr. by Meredith Weatherby. N. Y., Knopf, 1956; Tokyo, Tuttle, 1956; London, Secker and Warburg, 1957.
THE TEMPLE OF DAWN (The Sea of Fertility v.3) Tr. by E. Dale Saunders and Cecilia Segawa Seigle. N. Y., Knopf, 1973.
THE TEMPLE OF THE GOLDEN PAVILION Tr. by Ivan Morris. N. Y., Knopf, 1958; Tokyo, Tuttle, 1959; London, Secker and Warburg, 1959.
THIRST FOR LOVE Tr. by Alfred H. Marks. N. Y.,

Knopf, 1969; Tokyo, Tuttle, 1970; London, Secker and Warburg, 1970.
TWILIGHT SUNFLOWER Tr. by Shigeho Shinozaki and Virgil A. Warren. Tokyo, Hokuseidô, 1958.

MORI ÔGAI　森　鷗外　(1862–1922)
MASTERPIECES OF JAPANESE POETRY ANCIENT AND MODERN Vigorous Feet. Tr. by Asatarô Miyamori. Tokyo, Taiseidô, 1936, 1956; N. Y., Greenwood, 1971.
MODERN JAPANESE LITERATURE The Wild Goose. Tr. by Burton Watson. Ed. by D. Keene. N. Y., Grove Press, 1956; Tokyo, Tuttle, 1957.
MODERN JAPANESE STORIES Under Reconstruction. Ed. and tr. by Ivan Morris. London, Spottiswoode, 1961; Tokyo, Tuttle, 1962.
MY LADY OF THE DANCE Tr. by F. W. Eastlake. Tokyo, Saiunkaku, 1906.
REPRESENTATIVE TALES OF JAPAN Cups. Tr. by Asatarô Miyamori. Tokyo, Sanseidô, 1914.
SANSHÔ DAYU AND OTHER STORIES Tr. by Tsutomu Fukuda. Tokyo, Hokuseidô, 1952.
THE HEART IS ALONE Takasebune. Tr. by Garland W. Paschal. Ed. by R. McKinnon. Tokyo, Hokuseidô, 1957.
THE LANGUAGE OF LOVE The Girl Who Danced. Tr. by Leon Zolbrod. N. Y., Bantam Books, 1964.
THE WILD GEESE Tr. by Kingo Ochiai and Sanford Goldstein. Tokyo, Tuttle, 1959.
THE WRITING OF IDIOMATIC ENGLISH The Wild Goose. Tr. by S. G. Brickley. Tokyo, Kenkyûsha, 1951.
TOKYO PEOPLE: THREE STORIES FROM THE JAPANESE As If. Tr. by G. M. Sinclair and Kazo Suita. Tokyo, Keibunkan, 1925.
TREASURY OF WORLD LITERATURE The Pier. Tr. by Torao Taketomo. Ed. by D. D. Runes. N. Y., Philosophical Library, 1956.

NAGAI KAFÛ　永井　荷風　(1879–1959)
A STRANGE TALE FROM EAST OF THE RIVER AND OTHER STORIES Tr. by Edward Seidensticker. Tokyo, Tuttle, 1971.
JAPANESE LITERATURE NEW AND OLD Pleasure. Tr. by Ryôzô Matsumoto. Tokyo, Hokuseidô, 1961.
KAFU THE SCRIBBLER A Strange Tale from East of the River. Tr. by Edward Seidensticker. Stanford Univ. Press, 1965.
MODERN JAPANESE LITERATURE The River Sumida. Ed. and tr. by Donald Keene. N. Y., Grove Press, 1956; Tokyo, Tuttle, 1957.
MODERN JAPANESE STORIES Hydrangea. Tr. by Edward Seidensticker Ed. by I. Morris. London, Spottiswoode, 1961; Tokyo, Tuttle, 1962.
REPRESENTATIVE TALES OF JAPAN The Fox. Tr. by Asatarô Miyamori. Tokyo, Sankô Shoin, 1917.
THE WRITING OF IDIOMATIC ENGLISH The Two Wives. Tr. by S. G. Brickley. Tokyo, Kenkyûsha, 1951.
TREASURY OF WORLD LITERATURE The Bill-Collecting. Tr. by Torao Taketomo. Ed. by D. D. Runes. N. Y., Philosophical Library, 1956.

NATSUME SÔSEKI　夏目　漱石　(1867–1916)
ANTHOLOGY OF HAIKU, ANCIENT AND MODERN 26 Haiku. Tr. by Asatarô Miyamori. Tokyo, Maruzen, 1932.
BOTCHAN Tr. by Yasotarô Mori. Tokyo, Kinshodô, 1963.
BOTCHAN Tr. by Umeji Sasaki. Tokyo, Tuttle, 1968; London, Prentice-Hall, 1968.
BOTCHAN Tr. by Alan Turney. Tokyo, Kôdansha, 1972.
GRASS ON THE WAYSIDE Tr. by Edwin McClellan. Chicago, Univ. of Chicago Press, 1969; Tokyo, Tuttle, 1971.
HAIKU POEMS ANCIENT AND MODERN The Bay of Waka-no-Ura. Tr. by Asatarô Miyamori. Tokyo, Maruzen, 1940.
I AM A CAT Tr. by Kan'ichi Andô. Tokyo, Hattori Shoten, 1906.
I AM A CAT Tr. by Katsue Shibata and Motonari Kai. Tokyo, Kenkyûsha, 1961.
KOKORO Tr. by Ineko Satô. Tokyo, Kenkyûsha, 1941.
KOKORO Tr. by Edwin McClellan. Chicago, Regnery, 1957; London, Peter Owen, 1967; Tokyo, Tuttle, 1969.
KUSAMAKURA AND BUNCHO Tr. by Umeji Sasaki. Tokyo, Iwanami, 1927.
LIGHT AND DARKNESS Tr. by V. H. Viglielmo. London, Peter Owen, 1971.
MODERN JAPANESE LITERATURE Botchan. Tr. by Burton Watson. One Haiku. Tr. by H. G. Henderson. Ed. by D. Keene. N. Y., Grove Press, 1956; Tokyo, Tuttle, 1957.
MON Tr. by Francis Mathy. Tokyo, Tuttle, 1972.
REPRESENTATIVE TALES OF JAPAN Dream. Tr. by Asatarô Miyamori. Tokyo, Sankô Shoten, 1917.
TEN NIGHTS' DREAMS AND OUR CAT'S GRAVE Tr. by Sankichi Hara and Dofu Shirai. Tokyo, Seitô Shorin, 1934.
THE THREE-CORNERED WORLD (KUSA MAKURA) Tr. by Alan Turney. Tokyo, Tuttle, 1965; London, Peter Owen, 1965; Chicago, Regnery, 1967.
THE WAYFARER Tr. by Beongcheon Yu. Detroit, Wayne State Univ. Press, 1967; Tokyo, Tuttle, 1969.
THE WRITING OF IDIOMATIC ENGLISH The Paddy Bird. Tr. by S. G. Brickley. Tokyo, Kenkyûsha, 1951.
TREASURY OF WORLD LITERATURE Our Cat's Grave. Tr. by Sankichi Hara and Dofu Shirai. Ed. by D. D. Runes. N. Y., Philosophical Library, 1956.
UNHUMAN TOUR (KUSA MAKURA) Tr. by Kazutomo Takahashi. Tokyo, Japan Times, 1927.
WITHIN MY GLASS DOORS Tr. by Iwao Matsuhara and E. T. Iglehart. Tokyo, Shinseidô, 1928.

NISHIDA KITARÔ　西田幾多郎　(1870–1945)
ART AND MORALITY Tr. by David A. Dilworth and Valda H. Viglielmo. Honolulu, East-West Center Press, 1973.
A STUDY OF GOOD Tr. by V. H. Viglielmo. Tokyo, Japanese Government Printing Bureau, 1960.
FUNDAMENTAL PROBLEMS OF PHILOSOPHY Tr. by D. Dilworth. Tokyo, Sophia Univ. Press, 1970.

INTELLIGIBILITY AND THE PHILOSOPHY OF NOTHINGNESS Tr. by R. Schinzinger. Honolulu, East-West Center Press, 1966.

ÔOKA SHÔHEI　大岡　昇平　(b. 1909)
FIRES ON THE PLAIN Tr. by Ivan Morris. N. Y., Knopf, 1957; London, Secker and Warburg, 1957; Tokyo, Tuttle, 1967; London, Transworld, 1959; London, Panther, 1968; Harmondsworth, Penguin Books, 1969.
SOLIDARITY Prisoner of War. Tr. by Sakuko Matsui. v. 2, no. 7, 1967.

SHIGA NAOYA　志賀　直哉　(1883–1971)
EMINENT AUTHORS OF CONTEMPORARY JAPAN The Patron Saint of a Shop-Boy and other 4 stories. Tr. by Eric S. Bell and Eiji Ukai. v.1, Tokyo, Kaitakusha, 1930.
JAPANESE LITERATURE NEW AND OLD Han's Crime. Tr. by Ryôzô Matsumoto. Tokyo, Hokuseidô, 1961.
JAPANESE SHORT STORIES Han's Crime. Tr. by Ivan Morris. Tokyo, Japan Pub. Trading Co., 1960.
MODERN JAPANESE LITERATURE Han's Crime. Tr. by Ivan Morris. At Kinosaki. Tr. by Edward Seidensticker. Ed. by D. Keene. N. Y., Grove Press, 1956; Tokyo, Tuttle, 1957.
MODERN JAPANESE STORIES Seibei's Gourds. Ed. and tr. by Ivan Morris. London, Spottiswoode, 1961; Tokyo, Tuttle, 1962.
SELECTIONS FROM MODERN JAPANESE WRITERS An Old Man. Ed. and tr. by Arther L. Sadler. Sydney, Australian Medical Pub. Co., 1943.
THE HEART IS ALONE The Patron Saint. Tr. by Michael Y. Matsudaira. Ed. by R. McKinnon. Tokyo, Hokuseidô, 1957.
THE MENTOR BOOK OF MODERN ASIAN LITERATURE The Patron Saint. Tr. by Michael Y. Matsudaira. Ed. by D. B. Shimer. N. Y., New American Library, 1969.
THE WRITING OF IDIOMATIC ENGLISH Death of a Hermit Crab. Tr. by S. G. Brickley. Tokyo, Kenkyûsha, 1951.

SHIMAZAKI TÔSON　島崎　藤村　(1872–1943)
AN ANTHOLOGY OF MODERN JAPANESE POETRY Like a Fox. A Coconut. Ed. and tr. by Ichirô Kôno and Rikutarô Fukuda. Tokyo, Kenkyûsha, 1957.
THESIS An integral translation with an introduction of Iye by Shimazaki Tôson. Univ. of Pennsylvania, 1971
EMINENT AUTHORS OF CONTEMPORARY JAPAN Awakening Tr. by Eric S. Bell and Eiji Ukai. v. 1, Tokyo, Kaitakusha, 1930.
MODERN JAPANESE LITERATURE The Broken Commandment. (Synopsis) Tr. by Edward Seidensticker. Song on Traveling the Chikuma River. Tr. by Donald Keene. Ed. by D. Keene. N. Y., Grove Press, 1956; Tokyo, Tuttle, 1957.
MODERN JAPANESE POETRY By the Old Castle of Komoro. (part) Tr. by Donald Keene. Ann Arbor, Center for Japanese Studies, 1964.

PAULOWNIA: SEVEN STORIES FROM CONTEMPORARY JAPANESE WRITERS A Domestic Animal and other story. Tr. by Torao Taketomo. N. Y., Duffield, 1918.
REPRESENTATIVE TALES OF JAPAN Should She Have Told Him? Tr. by Asatarô Miyamori. Tokyo, Sankô Shoten, 1917.
THE BROKEN COMMANDMENT Tr. by Kenneth Strong. Tokyo, Univ. of Tokyo Press, 1974.
THE PENGUIN BOOK OF JAPANESE VERSE By the Old Castle at Komoro. Song of Travel on the Chikuma River. Coconut. Tr. by Geoffrey Bownas and Anthony Thwaite. Harmondsworth, Penguin Books, 1964.
THE POETRY OF LIVING JAPAN Otsuta. In the Birdless Country. Crafty Fox. First Love. A Coconut. Tr. by Takamichi Ninomiya and D. J. Enright. London, Murray, 1957.
THE WRITING OF IDIOMATIC ENGLISH First Journey. Tr. by S. G. Brickley. Tokyo, Kenkyûsha, 1951.

TANIZAKI JUN'ICHIRÔ　谷崎潤一郎 (1886–1965)
A PORTRAIT OF SHUNKIN Tr. by Howard S. Hibbett. Tokyo, Hara Shobô, 1965.
ASIKARI AND THE STORY OF SHUNKIN Tr. by Roy Humpherson and Hajime Okita. Tokyo, Hokuseidô, 1936; Westport, Greenwood, 1970.
DIARY OF A MAD OLD MAN Tr. by Howard Hibbett. N. Y., Knopf, 1965; London, Secker and Warburg, 1966; Tokyo, Tuttle, 1967.
EMINENT AUTHORS OF CONTEMPORARY JAPAN Okuni and Gohei. (v. 2) The White Fox. (v. 1) Tr. by Eric S. Bell and Eiji Ukai. Tokyo, Kaitakusha, 1931.
MODERN JAPANESE STORIES Tattoo. Tr. by Ivan Morris. London, Spottiswoode, 1961; Tokyo, Tuttle, 1962.
REPRESENTATIVE TALES OF JAPAN The Young Tattooer. Tr. by Asatarô Miyamori. Tokyo, Sankô Shoten, 1917.
SEVEN JAPANESE TALES A Portrait of Shunkin and other 6 stories. Tr. by Howard S. Hibbett. N. Y., Knopf, 1963; London, Secker and Warburg, 1964.
SOME PREFER NETTLES Tr. by Edward Seidensticker. N. Y., Knopf, 1955; London, Secker and Warburg, 1955; Tokyo, Tuttle, 1955.
THE KEY Tr. by Howard Hibbett. N. Y., Knopf, 1961; London, Secker and Warburg, 1961; Tokyo, Tuttle, 1962; N. Y., New American Library, 1962.
THE MAKIOKA SISTERS Tr. by E. G. Seidensticker. N. Y., Knopf, 1957; Tokyo, Tuttle, 1958.
THE WRITING OF IDIOMATIC ENGLISH The House Where I Was Born. Tr. by S. G. Brickley. Tokyo, Kenkyûsha, 1951.

TOKUDA SHÛSEI　徳田　秋声　(1871–1943)
MODERN JAPANESE STORIES Order of the White Paulownia. Tr. by Ivan Morris. London, Spottiswoode, 1961; Tokyo, Tuttle, 1962.
REPRESENTATIVE TALES OF JAPAN The Shoiage. Tr. by Asatarô Miyamori. Tokyo, Sankô Shoten, 1917.

WATSUJI TETSURÔ　和辻　哲郎　(1889–1960)
A CLIMATE (FÛDO) Tr. by Geoffrey Bownas.

Tokyo, Japanese Government Printing Bureau, 1961.
CLIMATE AND CULTURE (FÛDO) Tr. by Geoffrey
Bownas. Tokyo, Hokuseidô, 1971.

YOSHIYUKI JUNNOSUKE　吉行淳之介　(b. 1924)

JAPAN P. E. N. NEWS *Rusted Sea*. Tr. by Warren
Carlisle. no. 20, Sept. 1967.
NEW WRITING IN JAPAN *Sudden Shower*. Tr. by
Geoffrey Bownas. Harmondsworth, Penguin Books,
1972.

Editor's Postscript

The purpose of this book is not to serve merely as an explanation of Japanese literature, but rather, as the title indicates, this is an invitation to consider the works of Japan's literature from the ancient classics to contemporary writings through the keen perceptions of many internationally noted interpreters and specialists of the Japan scene. The editors have compiled this book for those persons throughout the world who have a deep interest in Japan and who are inquisitive about achieving more than just a superficial cultural interchange between their own country and Japan.

The contents of this book have been written by forty writers from twelve different countries, each in accordance with his own interest in the literary works of Japan or specific Japanese writers. In these forty compositions the reader will find a wealth of beautiful and artistic expressions as well as a scholarly and factual approach by all of the writers in describing the authors or works in which they have a strong interest. In addition to the excellent insights afforded by these forty writers, the editors have prepared brief background notes to assist the reader in understanding some of the historic and biographic materials presented in this volume.

It is our expectation that as a result of reading this book our overseas readers will have a valuable key for not only appreciating Japanese literature more fully, but they will also have a better understanding of the Japanese people as well. As for the Japanese readers, we hope that as a result of the fresh insights and interpretations presented here by foreign writers, this book will serve as a rediscovery of their own Japanese literary heritage.

We would like the readers to know that without the support and encouragement of many friends throughout the world the preparation of this book would not have been possible. We deeply appreciate the efforts of all those who contributed to this volume, and as a result of their friendship and cooperation we hope that many new friends will flourish and develop from among the readers.

MURAKAMI HYÔYE
Japan Culture Institute

〈CHRONOLOGICAL TABLE〉

JAPAN	JAPANESE LITERATURE	ERA	CHINA	OCCIDENTAL LITERATURE	OCCIDENT
Jōmon Period		B. C.	The Book of Songs The Scripture of Documents The Book of Changes The Chronicles of Lu The Analects of Confucius [Chin] SHIN HUANG TI	HOMER Iliad, Odyssey HERODOTUS History	Persian War
Yayoi Period		A. D.	[Han] SSU-MA CH'IEN Shih Chi (Records of the Historian) Han Shu (The History of the Former Han Dynasty) CHEN SHOU San Kuo Chih (The Three Kingdoms)	J. CAESAR Gallic Wars	Roman Empire founded
Yamato Court unified the country				TACITUS Germania PLUTARCH Lives New Testament	
Buddhism introduced					Roman Empire divided
Japanese Envoy to Sui, Tang			[Sui] [Tang]		
Nara Period	Kojiki (Records of Ancient Matters) Mannyōshū (Ten Thousand Poems) 空海 KŪKAI Sangō Shiiki (Instructions in the Three Teachings)	—700	An Lu-shan Rebellion LI PO Poems of Li Po TU FU Poems of Tu Fu	Chanson de Roland (France)	CHARLEMAGNE
Heian Period		—800			
SAICHŌ, KŪKAI to Tang Kana Syllabary developed	Taketori Monogatari (The Tale of the Bamboo-Cutter)	—900			
	清少納言 SEI SHŌNAGON Makura no Sōshi (The Pillow Book) 紫式部 MURASAKI SHIKIBU Genji Monogatari (The Tale of Genji) Konjaku Monogatari (Tales of Ages Ago)	—1000	[Sung]	Nibelungenlied (Germany)	Holy Roman Empire founded
Hōgen Rebellion Heiji Rebellion		—1100		M. POLO Description of the World	Paris University Oxford University First Crusade
MINAMOTO NO YORITOMO Kamakura Shogunate	Heike Monogatari (Tales of the Heike)	—1200			Cambridge University MARCO POLO to Yuan
Spread of Popular Buddhist Sects	Tannishō (The Analects of Shinran)	—1300	[Yuan]	DANTE ALIGHIERI Divine Comedy G. BOCCACCIO Decameron	
ASHIKAGA TAKAUJI Muromachi Shogunate	吉田 兼好 YOSHIDA KENKŌ Tsurezuregusa (Essays in Idleness) Soga Monogatari (The Tale of the Soga Brothers)	—1400	[Ming] SHIH NAI-AN Shui Hu Chuan (All Men Are Brothers)	G. CHAUCER The Canterbury Tales	Renaissance GUTENBERG: printing machine Eastern Roman Empire fell COLUMBUS to West Indies
	世阿弥 ZE-AMI				
Sengoku (Warlike) Period	Tauye Zōshi (A Collection of Rice-Planters' Songs)	—1500	WU CH'ENG-EN Hsi Yu Chi (The Adventures of a Monkey) Chin P'ing Mei (The Golden Lotus)	M. E. MONTAIGNE Essais W. SHAKESPEARE The Merchant of Venice	LUTHER: Reformation
guns, Christianity introduced	井原 西鶴 IHARA SAIKAKU Shokokubanashi (Tales from the Several Provinces) 松尾 芭蕉 MATSUO BASHŌ Oku no Hosomichi (The Narrow Inland Roads) 近松門左衛門 CHIKAMATSU MONZAYEMON	—1600	[Ching]	M. DE CERVANTES Don Quixote MOLIÈRE Le Misanthrope B. PASCAL Pensées	Thirty Years War Puritan Revolution 'Glorious' Revolution
TOKUGAWA IYEYASU Edo Shogunate	Kokusen'ya Kassen (The Battles of Coxinga) 与謝 蕪村 YOSA BUSON 上田 秋成 UYEDA AKINARI Ugetsu Monogatari (Tales of Moonlight and Rain)	—1700		J. SWIFT Gulliver's Travels J. W. GOETHE Die Leiden des Jungen Werthers	War of Austrian Succession Declaration of Independence French Revolution
PERRY to Uraga		—1800	Opium War Taiping Rebellion	F. SCHILLER Wilhelm Tell STENDHAL Le Rouge et le Noir H. DE BALZAC Comédie Humaine W. WHITMAN Leaves of Grass P. C. BAUDELAIRE Les Fleurs du Mal V. M. HUGO Les Misérables F. M. DOSTOEVSKI Crime and Punishment	Queen VICTORIA Opium War Civil War

Year	World History	World Literature	China / Asia	Japanese Literature	Japanese History
1870	Commune of Paris	C. L. N. TOLSTOI *War and Peace*; M. TWAIN *The Adventures of Tom Sawyer*; H. IBSEN *A Doll's House*			Meiji Restoration; Satsuma Rebellion
1880		G. DE MAUPASSANT *Une Vie*	Sino-French War	森 鷗外 MORI OGAI *Maihime (The Girl Who Danced)*	Constitution promulgated
1890			Sino-Japanese War	樋口 一葉 HIGUCHI ICHIYŌ *Takekurabe (Growing Up)*; 正岡 子規 MASAOKA SHIKI *Utayomi ni Atauru Sho (Exhortations to Tanka Poets)*	Sino-Japanese War
1900	Spanish-American War; Nobel Prizes (first)	E. ROSTAND *Cyrano de Bergerac*; A. P. CHEKHOV *The Three Sisters*; M. GORKI *The Lower Depths*; H. HESSE *Unterm Rad*; A. GIDE *La Porte Étroite*	Boxers' Rebellion	永井 荷風 NAGAI KAFŪ *Amerika Monogatari (Stories from America)*; 夏目 漱石 NATSUME SŌSEKI *Sorekara (And Then)*	Anglo-Japanese Alliance; Russo-Japanese War
1910		R. ROLLAND *Jean Christophe*; M. PROUST *À la Recherche du Temps Perdu*	Chinese Revolution / Republic of China founded / Ching fell	西田幾多郎 NISHIDA KITARŌ *Zen no Kenkyū (A Study of Good)*; 石川 啄木 ISHIKAWA TAKUBOKU *Kanashiki Gangu (Sad Toys)*; 芥川龍之介 AKUTAGAWA RYŪNOSUKE *Rashōmon*	Kōtoku High Treason Affair; Rice Riots
1920	World War I; Russian Revolution; League of Nations; MUSSOLINI came to power	T. S. ELIOT *The Waste Land*; D. H. LAWRENCE *Lady Chatterley's Lover*; E. M. HEMINGWAY *A Farewell to Arms*	Lu Hsün *The True Story of AhQ*	志賀 直哉 SHIGA NAOYA *An'ya Kōro (Journey in Darkness)*; 川端 康成 KAWABATA YASUNARI *Izu no Odoriko (The Izu Dancer)*; 島崎 藤村 SHIMAZAKI TŌSON *Yoakemaye (Before the Dawn)*	Kantō Earthquake Disaster; Law for Maintenance of the Public Peace; Law for Universal Suffrage
1930	World Depression; HITLER came to power; New Deal (U.S.A.)	W. H. FAULKNER *Sanctuary*; M. MITCHELL *Gone with the Wind*	Manchurian Incident; Marco Polo Bridge Incident	和辻 哲郎 WATSUJI TETSURŌ *Fūdo (Climate and Culture)*; 井伏 鱒二 IBUSE MASUJI *Tajinko Mura (Tajinko Village)*	Manchurian Incident
1940	World War II; Unconditional Surrender (Germany); United Nations Declaration of Human Rights	J. P. SARTRE *Les Chemins de la Liberté*; A. CAMUS *L'Étranger*	People's Republic of China founded	徳田 秋声 TOKUDA SHUSEI; 谷崎潤一郎 TANIZAKI JUNICHIRŌ *Sasame Yuki (The Makioka Sisters)*; 太宰 治 DAZAI OSAMU *Shayō (The Setting Sun)*; 三島由紀夫 MISHIMA YUKIO *Kamen no Kokuhaku (Confessions of a Mask)*	Pacific War; Unconditional Surrender; New Constitution promulgated
1950	Artificial Satellite (U.S.S.R.)			大岡 昇平 ŌOKA SHŌHEI *Nobi (Fires on the Plain)*; 吉行淳之介 YOSHIYUKI JUNNOSUKE *Shūu (Sudden Shower)*	San Francisco Peace Treaty signed; joined United Nations
1960	First Arrival to the Moon (U.S.A.)	A. I. SOLZHENITSYN *One Day in the Life of Ivan Denisovich*	Great Cultural Revolution	安部 公房 ABE KŌBŌ *Suna no Onna (Woman in the Dunes)*; 遠藤 周作 ENDŌ SHŪSAKU *Chinmoku (Silence)*	
1970				開高 健 KAIKŌ TAKESHI *Natsu no Yami (Darkness in Summer)*	Okinawan Reversion